CGP

BTEC FIRST
Business
Study & Exam Practice

This book is for anyone doing **BTEC Level 2 First Award in Business**.
It covers the examined unit of the course — **Unit 2**.

All the **important topics** are explained in a clear, straightforward
way to help you get all the marks you can in the exam.

It's full of **useful practice questions** to help you get to grips with all
the essential information, as well as a **CD-ROM** containing **two** complete
practice papers to make sure you're fully prepared.

What CGP is all about

Our sole aim here at CGP is to produce the highest
quality books — carefully written, immaculately presented
and dangerously close to being funny.

Then we work our socks off to get them
out to you — at the cheapest possible prices.

Published by CGP

Editors:
Rachel Grocott
Lucy Loveluck
Holly Poynton
Sabrina Robinson

Contributor:
Murray Hamilton

ISBN: 978 1 84762 473 4

With thanks to Glenn Rogers for the proofreading.

With thanks to Lorna Aspden for the proofreading and reviewing.

With thanks to Laura Jakubowski for the copyright research.

Printed by Elanders Ltd, Newcastle upon Tyne.
Clipart from Corel®

Based on the classic CGP style created by Richard Parsons.

Contents

Exam Tips

This book is for anyone studying BTEC First Award in Business.

Here is what will happen...

There are four units in this course.

Unit 1	Unit 1 will be assessed by your teacher. Your teacher will set you an assignment.
Unit 2	For Unit 2, you'll have to do an onscreen exam.
Two other units	Your teacher will choose two units from units 3–8. Your teacher will set you assignments. These will be assessed by your teacher.

Unit 2 is worth 25% of the total marks.

How to use this book

This book is to help you with the Unit 2 exam.

1) The revision pages have all the facts you need to learn.
   - Read a page.
   - Cover it up.
   - Scribble down what you remember.
   - Do this until you can write down all the key points on the page.

2) Now use the question pages to test you really know your stuff.

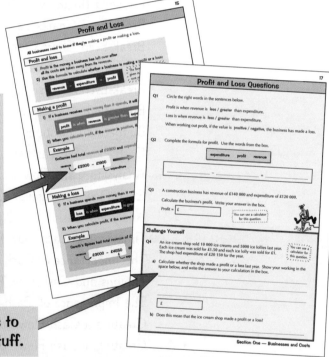

3) When you've worked through all the pages do the two practice exams on the CD.

Top exam tips

1) Make sure you read all the information given to you in the question.
2) Look at the number of marks on offer to give you an idea of how much to write.
3) If you are asked to calculate something, make sure you show your working.
4) Make sure you understand what the question is asking you to do.
   Take a look at the guide on the next two pages for some handy tips.

Exam Tips

Types of exam question

Certain words in an exam question tell you what to do. It's a good idea to learn what these words mean. Then they won't be able to trip you up.

1) Calculate
Do some maths. Use the working box to show your calculations.

A business bakes and sells cakes.
Each cake retails for £1.50.
The business sold 40 000 cakes last year.

Question 1 of 19

Calculate the total revenue for the business. (2)

Type your answer in the box.

£ 60 000

You may use the working box to show your calculations.

40 000 × £1.50 = £60 000

2) Identify
Show or select something.

Chris makes and sells deckchairs.

Question 2 of 19

This is his break-even chart.

a) Identify the break-even point on this chart. (1)

Drag the **X** onto the chart to show the break-even point.

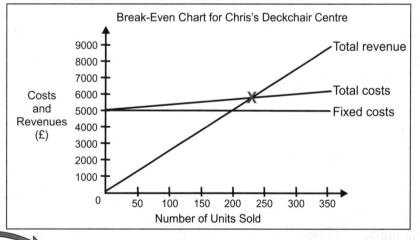

Break-Even Chart for Chris's Deckchair Centre

3) Explain
Give a reason for something.

b) Explain an advantage of drawing break-even charts. (2)

Type your answer in the box.

So businesses know how many units they need to sell to start making a profit.

4

Exam Tips

Olly is analysing data for his business.

He looks at this extract from his statement of financial position (balance sheet).

Question 3 of 19

4) Define
Say what the word means.

	£	£
Fixed assets		
Delivery van		5000

a) (Define) the term fixed asset.   (1)

Type your answer in the box.

A fixed asset is something a business owns long-term, for example, a company vehicle or an office.

Olly has also started making an income statement (profit and loss account).

b) (Complete) the extract from Olly's income statement below. Use the words in the boxes to help you.   (3)

5) Complete
Add in the missing information. This often means doing some calculations to fill in the gaps.

Gross profit	Net profit	Total expenses

	£	£
Income from sales		15 000
Cost of sales	7500	
Gross profit		7500
Expenses		
Rent	1100	
Advertising	520	
Total expenses	1620	
Net profit		5880

6) Recommend
Suggest how something could be done.

c) (Recommend) one way Olly could increase his net profit.   (2)

Type your answer in the box.

Olly could try to reduce his cost of sales by finding a cheaper supplier.

Exam Tips

Business Costs

Costs are all the things a business spends its money on.

Start-up costs

1) Start-up costs are the costs a business pays out when they are first setting up.
2) They are usually things a business only has to pay for once.
3) For example, a new bakery would need to buy an oven.
4) They are things a business has to pay for before it can start trading.

Operating (running) costs

1) Operating costs are the things a business pays for on a regular basis.
2) They can also be called running costs.
3) Examples of running costs are rent, staff wages and raw materials.
4) Operating costs can be split into two types: fixed costs and variable costs.

Fixed costs

1) Fixed costs don't change depending on output. Output is the number of products made.
2) A business has to pay its fixed costs even if it produces nothing.
3) Rent is an example of a fixed cost. Even if a business produces nothing, the rent still has to be paid.
4) Other examples of fixed costs could be water bills and broadband costs.

Variable costs

1) Variable costs change depending on output.
2) Variable costs are the opposite of fixed costs.
3) Raw materials are an example of a variable cost.
4) If a business has to make more products, it will need more raw materials.
5) This means the amount spent on raw materials will increase.
6) Staff wages can be an example of a variable cost, but only when staff are paid directly according to what they produce.
7) For example, staff on a production line putting computers together.

Business Costs

Make sure you know all the different types of business costs.

Calculating variable costs

1) To work out a business's variable costs, you need to know the variable cost per unit.

2) 'Variable cost per unit' just means how much it costs to make each unit.

3) So, the variable cost of making a pair of trainers (a unit) would include the price of the raw materials (fabric and rubber) added to the labour costs (how much you paid someone to stitch the trainers together).

4) Once you know the variable cost per unit, use this formula to work out variable costs:

| variable cost per unit | x | number made/sold | = | variable costs |

Example

Pies R Us sells 800 pies a week with variable costs of £1.50 per pie.

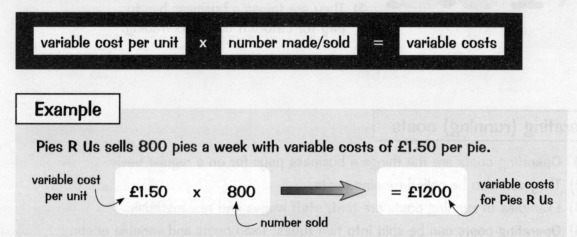

variable cost per unit → £1.50 x 800 → = £1200 variable costs for Pies R Us

number sold

Direct and indirect costs

Costs can also be split into direct costs or indirect costs.

Direct costs

1) Direct costs are expenses that directly relate to making a product.

2) For example, some staff wages and raw materials.

3) These costs are similar to variable costs (see p.5) because they change depending on how many units a business makes.

Indirect costs

1) Indirect costs are costs that can't be directly related to making a product.

2) Examples include management salaries, telephone bills and office rent.

3) These costs are similar to fixed costs (see p.5) because they are not affected by how many units the business produces.

Business Costs

Use this page to help you work out a business's total costs.

Total costs

1) Total costs are all of a business's costs added together.

2) You can work out the total costs using this formula:

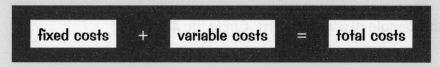

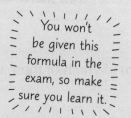

You won't be given this formula in the exam, so make sure you learn it.

Example 1

Pies R Us has fixed costs of £600 and variable costs of £1200 per week.

fixed costs per week — £600 + £1200 ➡ = £1800 total costs per week for Pies R Us
variable costs per week

3) The formula can also be written using 'direct' and 'indirect' costs:

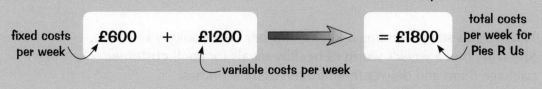

Example 2

Tom's TVs has indirect costs of £550 and direct costs of £1600 per week.

indirect costs per week — £550 + £1600 ➡ = £2150 total costs per week for Tom's TVs
direct costs per week

Practice Questions

1) True or false: a business has to pay start-up costs each year.

2) True or false: raw materials are an example of an indirect cost.

3) Give one example of an operating (running) cost.

4) If a business has fixed costs of £200 and variable costs of £800, what are its total costs?

Business Costs Questions

Q1 a) Which of these is an example of a **fixed cost**? Circle the answer.

> raw materials   office rent   production line staff wages   delivery costs

b) Which of these is an example of a **direct cost**? Circle the answer.

> staff training   raw materials   telephone bills   management salaries

Q2 Heather has started renting a kitchen for her new cookery business.
She will cook a week's worth of healthy meals for each customer,
package them and deliver them frozen to their homes.

Write down **two** examples of **variable costs** her business might have.

Example 1: ....

....

Example 2: ....

....

Q3 Eva is opening a new restaurant. These are some of her costs.

Which of these are **start-up costs** and which are **operating costs**?
Tick the correct boxes.

		start-up cost	operating cost
a)	A deposit on the restaurant building	☐	☐
b)	Staff wages	☐	☐
c)	Telephone bills	☐	☐
d)	Buying kitchen appliances	☐	☐

Business Costs Questions

Q4   Complete the formulas below. Use the words from the box.

total costs	variable costs	fixed costs

variable cost per unit × number made/sold   = ...

.... + variable costs   = ...

Q5 a)   Jake runs a cake shop.
He has **variable costs** of **£2** for each cake he sells.

If Jake sells **60** cakes in a week, what will his **variable costs** be?

Variable costs for 60 cakes =   £

b)   Jake's **fixed costs** for the week were **£550**.

Use your answer from part **a)** to calculate his **total costs** for the week.

Total costs for the week =   £

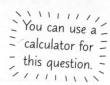
You can use a calculator for this question.

Q6   Chris is setting up a business that will sell cycling accessories online.
He has estimated the following monthly costs if he sells 1000 items.

- A **variable cost** of **£20** for each item he sells

- Total **fixed costs** of **£5000**

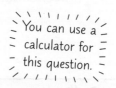
You can use a calculator for this question.

Fill in the gaps to complete the table.

	1000 items sold
Variable costs	£
Fixed costs	£
Total costs	£

Revenue

Revenue is really important for businesses. Without it, they wouldn't survive.

Revenue

1) Revenue is all the money that a business receives.
2) A business's main source of revenue is the money made from selling its products or services.
3) Without revenue a business wouldn't be able to pay its costs, and it would struggle to survive.

Other sources of revenue

1) Revenue doesn't just come from the sale of products and services.
2) Here are some other ways a business can make revenue.

Earning interest on savings

- Some businesses put money into high interest bank accounts.
- The interest this money earns makes more revenue for the business.

Investing in other businesses

- Businesses sometimes invest in other businesses.
- A business can buy shares in another business so that they own a part of the firm.
- This means they might get a share of any profit made by the other business, which creates more revenue for themselves.

A share is a small part of a business that can be bought by other people or businesses.

Selling or renting out resources

- A business may make revenue by selling or renting out things it doesn't need any more.
- It might sell or rent old equipment like machinery, or bigger things, like offices or land.

Revenue

So now you've learnt how businesses get revenue, you've got to learn how to calculate it.

Calculating revenue

Use this formula to work out a business's revenue:

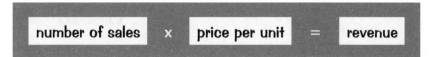

| number of sales | × | price per unit | = | revenue |

The formula for revenue isn't given in the exam, so make sure you learn it by heart.

Example 1

The Chilli Pepper Centre sold 650 pots of chilli jam in one month.
Each pot of chilli jam was sold for £4.50.

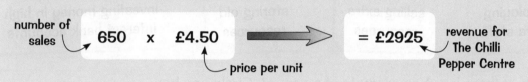

number of sales → 650 × £4.50 → = £2925 revenue for The Chilli Pepper Centre
price per unit

Example 2

PC Cumbria sold 210 computers in a month and 300 tablets.
Each computer was sold for £550 and each tablet was sold for £200.

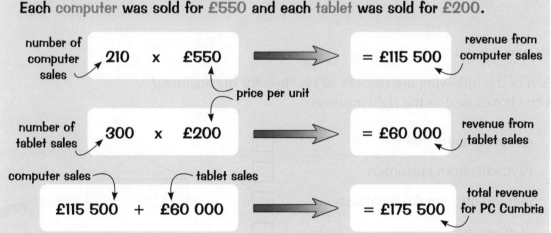

number of computer sales → 210 × £550 → = £115 500 revenue from computer sales
price per unit
number of tablet sales → 300 × £200 → = £60 000 revenue from tablet sales
computer sales ↘   tablet sales ↙
£115 500 + £60 000 → = £175 500 total revenue for PC Cumbria

Practice Questions

1) True or false: shares in businesses can only be bought by other businesses.

2) True or false: businesses can use high interest bank accounts to make more revenue.

3) What is revenue?

4) True or false: revenue = number of sales x price per unit

Revenue Questions

Q1   Circle the right words in the sentences below.

Revenue is all the money that a business **receives / pays out**.

Selling products or services / Selling land is the main source of revenue for a business.

Buying shares in another business / Renting a more expensive office can generate revenue.

Q2 a)   Which of these are examples of how a business can **make revenue**? Circle two boxes.

| employing extra staff | selling extra resources | storing old resources | investing money in high interest bank accounts |

b)   Which of these is **not** an example of **revenue**? Circle one box.

| advertising products | product sales | interest from savings |

Q3   Mark runs a hotel.

Which of the following are **sources of revenue** for his business?
Tick the boxes next to the right answers.

Advertising the hotel ☐

Payments from customers ☐

Ingredients to make breakfasts ☐

Staff wages ☐

Selling unwanted furniture ☐

No Vacancy

Q4   Read the sentences below. Circle true or false for each one.

Businesses can invest in other businesses to make more revenue. **true / false**

It is illegal for businesses to sell extra equipment to create revenue. **true / false**

A business would find it difficult to survive without revenue. **true / false**

Revenue Questions

Q5 Complete the formula used to calculate **revenue**. Choose the correct words from the boxes.

| profit | total costs | number of sales | cost of sales | price per unit |

revenue = ... x ....

Q6 a) Isaac makes and sells model planes.
Each model plane sells for **£10**.

Isaac sold **1000** model planes last year.

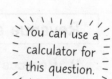

Calculate the **revenue** made from the sale of model planes last year.

Revenue from 1000 model planes = £

b) Isobel's business sells computers.
Each computer sells for **£250**.

Last year, her business sold **200 computers**.

Calculate the **revenue** made from the sale of computers last year.

Revenue from 200 computers = £

> You can use a calculator for this question.

Challenge Yourself

Q7 A bookshop sold **950** crime novels and **1100** cookbooks last year.
Each crime novel was sold for **£7.50** and each cookbook was sold for **£10**.

Calculate the **total revenue** from sales of crime novels and cookbooks last year.
Show your working in the space below.

....

....

....

....

> You can use a calculator for this question.

Total revenue = £

Expenditure

Businesses have to spend money to make money.

Expenditure

1) Expenditure is all the money that a business spends. Businesses have to spend money to succeed.
2) Expenditure can be split into two types: capital and revenue.

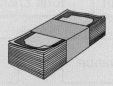

Capital expenditure

1) Capital expenditure is the money spent on assets that will be used by the business for a long time.
2) An example of capital expenditure is buying a fixed asset like new machinery.

Revenue expenditure

1) Revenue expenditure is the money spent on a business's day-to-day costs.
2) Staff wages, rent and utility bills are examples of revenue expenditure.

Utility bills are things like water, gas and electricity bills.

Overheads

1) Overheads are another type of expenditure.
2) Overheads are the everyday running costs of a business.
3) Overheads aren't directly linked with producing goods or services, but they need to be paid even if nothing is produced.
4) So, 'overheads' is just another way of saying 'indirect costs' (see p.6).
5) Examples of overheads are rent and electricity bills.

Practice Questions

1) True or false: an example of capital expenditure is the money spent on electricity bills.

2) Give one example of an overhead.

Profit and Loss

All businesses need to know if they're making a profit or making a loss.

Profit and loss

1) Profit is the money a business has left over after all its costs are taken away from its revenue.

2) Use this formula to calculate whether a business is making a profit or a loss:

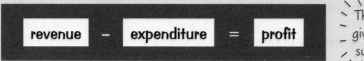

| revenue | − | expenditure | = | profit |

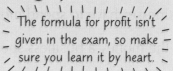

The formula for profit isn't given in the exam, so make sure you learn it by heart.

Making a profit

1) If a business receives more money than it spends, it will make a profit.

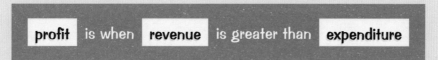

profit is when revenue is greater than expenditure

2) When you calculate profit, if the answer is positive, the business has made a profit.

Example

GoGames had total revenue of £2300 and expenditure of £1900.

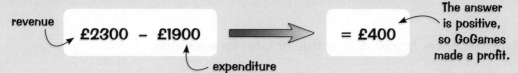

revenue £2300 − £1900 expenditure → = £400

The answer is positive, so GoGames made a profit.

Making a loss

1) If a business spends more money than it receives, it will make a loss.

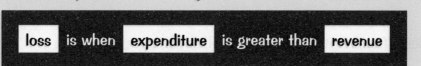

loss is when expenditure is greater than revenue

2) When you calculate profit, if the answer is negative, the business has made a loss.

Example

Gareth's Spices had total revenue of £3000 and expenditure of £4550.

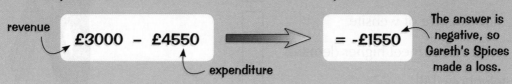

revenue £3000 − £4550 expenditure → = -£1550

The answer is negative, so Gareth's Spices made a loss.

Expenditure Questions

Q1   Fill in the missing words in the sentences below.

expenditure	succeed	rent	overheads

Businesses have to spend money in order to ....

All the money a business spends is known as ....

.... are an example of expenditure, and are also known as indirect costs.

An example of an overhead is ....

Q2   Which of these is an example of **expenditure**? Circle one box.

supplier discounts   money from sales   renting out old machinery   advertising

Q3   Read the sentences below. Circle true or false for each one.

Capital expenditure is money spent on assets that will be used for a long time. true / false

Revenue expenditure is the money spent on a business's day-to-day costs. true / false

Buying a new warehouse is an example of revenue expenditure. true / false

Q4   Dan's Desks makes office furniture. It has the following **expenditure**.

Identify which of these costs are **overheads**.
Tick the correct boxes.

rent ☐

wood to make the furniture ☐

maintenance of website ☐

extra staff to meet higher demand ☐

telephone bill ☐

Profit and Loss Questions

Q1 Circle the right words in the sentences below.

Profit is when revenue is less / **greater** than expenditure.

Loss is when revenue is **less** / greater than expenditure.

When working out profit, if the value is positive / **negative**, the business has made a loss.

Q2 Complete the formula for **profit**. Use the words from the box.

> expenditure   profit   revenue

.... – .... = ...

Q3 A construction business has revenue of **£140 000** and expenditure of **£120 000**.

Calculate the business's **profit**. Write your answer in the box.

Profit = £

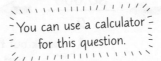

Challenge Yourself

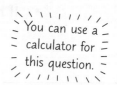

Q4 An ice cream shop sold **10 000** ice creams and **5000** ice lollies last year. Each ice cream was sold for **£1.50** and each ice lolly was sold for **£1**. The shop had expenditure of **£20 150** for the year.

a) Calculate whether the shop made a **profit** or a **loss** last year. Show your working in the space below, and write the answer to your calculation in the box.

....

....

....

£

b) Does this mean that the ice cream shop made a profit or a loss?

....

Breaking Even

Businesses use the break-even point to work out how much they must sell to make a profit.

Break-even point

1) The break-even point is when the amount of money spent on making the product is the same as the money made from selling the product.

2) At break-even point a business hasn't made either a profit or a loss.

Calculating break-even point

Use this formula to work out the break-even point:

> This line means 'divided by'.

$$\frac{\text{fixed costs}}{\text{selling price per unit} - \text{variable cost per unit}} = \text{break-even}$$

Example

- Usop's business makes sports bottles. They sell for £5 each.
  The business has fixed costs of £30 000. The variable cost per unit is £3.

$$\frac{30\ 000}{5-3} \quad \Rightarrow \quad \frac{30\ 000}{2} \quad \Rightarrow \quad 30\ 000 \div 2 \ = \ 15\ 000 \text{ bottles}$$

work out the bottom part first

- Usop must sell 15 000 sports bottles to cover the cost of making them.
- If he sells more than 15 000, he will make a profit.
- If he sells fewer than 15 000, he will make a loss.

Margin of safety

The margin of safety is the difference between the target or actual sales and the break-even point.

> Target sales is the amount of units a business aims to sell.

Example

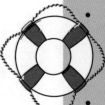

- Usop must sell 15 000 sports bottles to break even. However, Usop plans to sell 20 000 sports bottles. This means his margin of safety is:

$$20\ 000 - 15\ 000 = 5000$$

- This means Usop can sell 5000 fewer bottles than he expects before he risks making a loss.

Breaking Even

Break-even charts

1) A business's break-even point can be shown on a chart.

2) A break-even chart shows when a business will make a loss and when it will make a profit.

3) A break-even chart shows total revenue and total costs. It also shows fixed costs and the margin of safety.

4) The break-even point is where the lines for total revenue and total costs cross.

A break-even chart

Here's an example of a break-even chart.

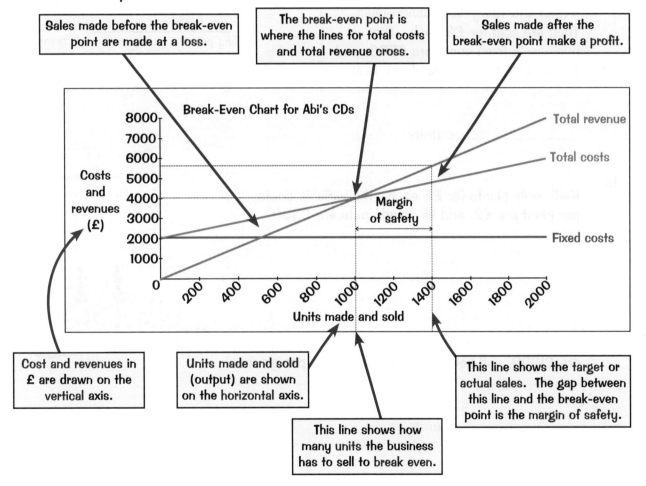

Sales made before the break-even point are made at a loss.

The break-even point is where the lines for total costs and total revenue cross.

Sales made after the break-even point make a profit.

Cost and revenues in £ are drawn on the vertical axis.

Units made and sold (output) are shown on the horizontal axis.

This line shows the target or actual sales. The gap between this line and the break-even point is the margin of safety.

This line shows how many units the business has to sell to break even.

Practice Questions

1) True or false: the break-even point is where the lines for fixed costs and total costs cross.

2) What is a break-even point?

3) How do you work out the margin of safety?

Breaking Even Questions

Q1 Are these sentences **true** or **false**? Tick the right boxes.

                                                 True **False**

a) At the break-even point, a business makes enough money to cover its costs. ☐ ☐

b) If a business meets the break-even point, it will make a profit. ☐ ☐

c) At the break-even point, a business hasn't made a profit or a loss. ☐ ☐

d) If a business breaks even, it will make a loss. ☐ ☐

Q2 Use the information in the boxes below to work out each business's **break-even point**.

a)

> 'Fresh and Tasty' sells sandwiches. They are sold for £3 each. The business's fixed costs are £500, and the variable cost per sandwich is £1.

$$\frac{\text{fixed costs}}{\dfrac{\text{selling price}}{\text{per unit}} - \dfrac{\text{variable cost}}{\text{per unit}}} = \text{break-even}$$

.... units

b)

> Keith sells plants for £5 each. His variable costs per plant are £2, and his fixed costs are £300.

You can use a calculator for this question.

.... units

c)

> Olana sells games for £10 each. Her fixed costs are £1200, and her variable costs are £4 per game.

.... units

Q3 What is the **margin of safety**? Tick the correct box.

a) The profit-making region of a break-even chart. ☐

b) The amount of sales a business must make to break even. ☐

c) The difference between the target or actual sales and the break-even point. ☐

Section Two — Planning for Success

Breaking Even Questions

Q4 **Circle** the right words to complete these sentences about break-even charts.

a) The **break-even point / vertical axis** shows how much a business must sell to cover its costs.

b) Sales made **before / after** the break-even point are made at a loss.

c) Sales made **before / after** the break-even point make a profit.

d) The break-even point is where the lines for **total costs / fixed costs** and total revenue cross.

e) The line for total costs always starts at **zero / the same point** where the fixed costs line starts.

Q5 Which sentences are correct? Circle **two** boxes.

| The horizontal axis shows the costs and revenues. | The vertical axis shows the costs and revenues. | The horizontal axis shows the units sold. | The vertical axis shows the units sold. |

Q6 Use the words below to label this **break-even chart**.

| break-even point | target or actual sales | margin of safety | units sold |

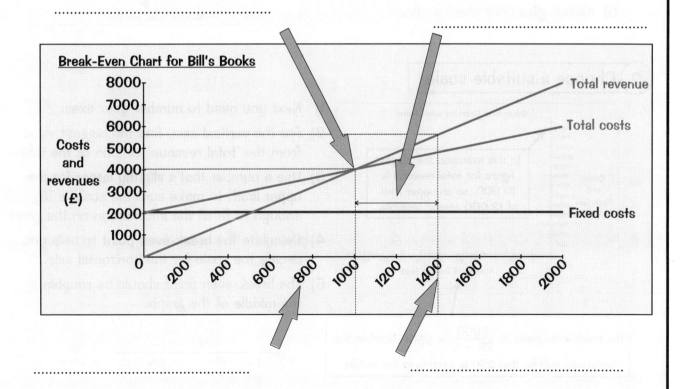

Break-Even Chart for Bill's Books

Drawing Break-Even Charts

These pages will show you how to draw your very own break-even chart. Lucky you.

Information for break-even charts

1) Here's an example of how to draw a break-even chart from a table of information.

2) Lara Leveret sells rabbits. Her fixed costs are £5000. Her variable costs are £5 a rabbit. She sells each rabbit for £25.

number of units (rabbits) sold	variable costs (£) (£5 per unit sold, so £5×units sold)	fixed costs (£)	total costs (£) (variable costs+fixed costs)	total revenue (£) (£25 per unit, so £25×units sold)
200	1000	5000	6000	5000
250	1250	5000	6250	6250
300	1500	5000	6500	7500
350	1750	5000	6750	8750
400	2000	5000	7000	10 000

1) Draw and label the axes

1) You can use the information in the table above to draw a break-even chart.

2) Start by drawing and labelling the axes.

3) The vertical axis is labelled 'Costs and Revenues'. It is measured in £.

4) The horizontal axis shows the number of units sold.

5) Always give your chart a title.

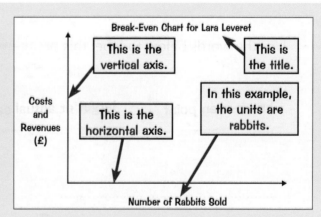

2) Choose a suitable scale

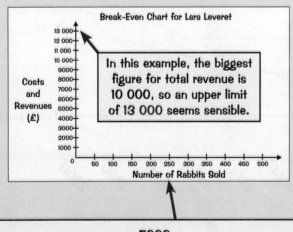

1) Next you need to number your axes.

2) For the vertical axis, find the biggest value from the 'total revenue' column of the table.

3) Use a number that's slightly larger for the upper limit, to make sure the scale is big enough to fit all the information on the graph.

4) Calculate the break-even point to help you decide the scale for the horizontal axis.

5) The break-even point should be roughly in the middle of the graph.

The break-even point is: $\frac{5000}{25-5} = 250$. Number the horizontal axis so that 250 is roughly in the middle.

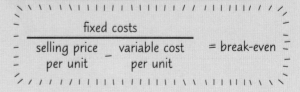

$$\frac{\text{fixed costs}}{\frac{\text{selling price}}{\text{per unit}} - \frac{\text{variable cost}}{\text{per unit}}} = \text{break-even}$$

Drawing Break-Even Charts

③ Draw the 'Total revenue' line

1) To draw the 'Total revenue' line, use the figures for 'number of units sold' and 'total revenue' from the table of information on p.22.

2) Find the highest values for each of these in the table. So in this example, you'd use 400 rabbits and £10 000.

3) Trace your finger up from 400 on the horizontal axis, and across from 10 000 on the vertical axis. Mark where these two values meet with a small cross.

4) Draw a straight line between this cross and the bottom left-hand corner of the graph at zero. Label this line 'Total revenue'.

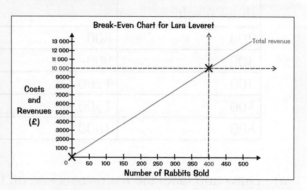

④ Draw the 'Fixed costs' and 'Total costs' lines

1) Draw the lines for 'Fixed costs' and 'Total costs' in a similar way.

2) The 'Fixed costs' line should be horizontal because fixed costs don't increase with sales.

3) To draw the 'Fixed costs' line, find the 'fixed costs' figure from the table. Draw a horizontal line starting from that point on the vertical axis.

4) Next, draw the 'Total costs' line. Plot a point using the largest pair of figures from the 'number of units sold' and 'total costs' column from the table.

5) Draw a straight line between this point and the point where the 'Fixed costs' line starts on the vertical axis. The 'Total costs' line never starts at zero.

6) If the lines for 'Total revenue' and 'Total costs' cross at the break-even point, your chart is probably correct.

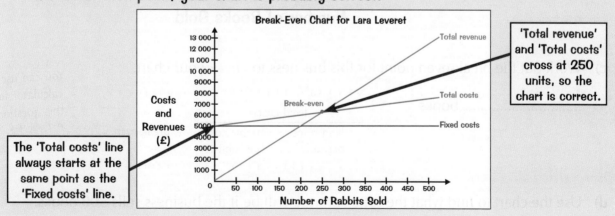

'Total revenue' and 'Total costs' cross at 250 units, so the chart is correct.

The 'Total costs' line always starts at the same point as the 'Fixed costs' line.

Practice Question

1) True or false: the 'total costs' line always starts at zero.

Drawing Break-Even Charts Questions

Q1) This table contains information about a bookshop. The shop's fixed costs are £700. The variable costs are £3 per book. Each book sells for £5.

Number of units (books) sold	Variable costs (£)	Fixed costs (£)	Total costs (£)
200	600	700	1300
300	900	700	1600
400	1200	700	1900
500	1500	700	2200
600	1800	700	2500

a) Draw and label the **fixed costs line** on the break-even chart below.

b) Draw and label the **total costs line** on the break-even chart below.

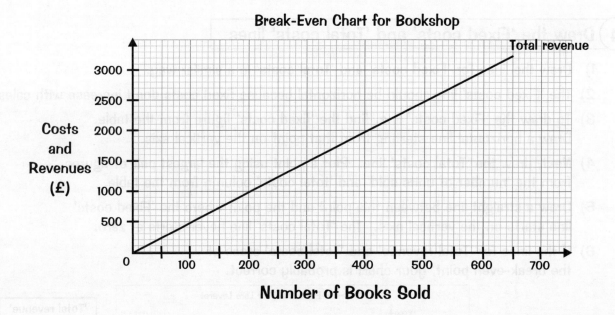

Break-Even Chart for Bookshop

c) Work out the break-even point for this business to **check** your chart.

.... books

$$\frac{\text{fixed costs}}{\text{selling price per unit} - \text{variable cost per unit}} = \text{break-even}$$

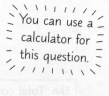

You can use a calculator for this question.

d) Use the chart to find what the **total revenue** will be if the business sells **500** books.

£ ....

e) Use the chart to find out **how many books** the business must sell in order to make **£3000** of **revenue**.

.... books

Drawing Break-Even Charts Questions

Challenge Yourself

Q2) Mamta makes and sells garden gnomes. They are **sold** for £8 each. Her **fixed costs** are £1500, and the **variable cost** per gnome is £3.

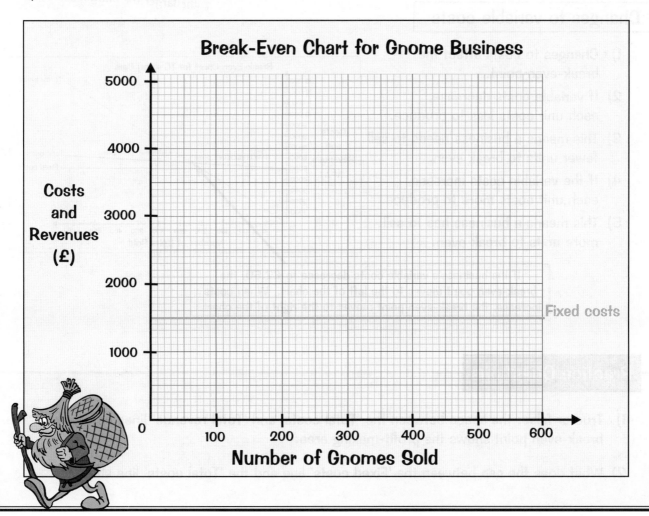

You can use a calculator for this question.

a) Fill in the missing information to **complete** the table.

Number of units sold	Variable costs (£)	Fixed costs (£)	Total costs (£)	Total revenue (£)
200	600	1500	2100	1600
300	900	1500		
400		1500		
500		1500		
600	1800	1500	3300	4800

b) Work out Mamta's **break-even point**.

.... gnomes

$$\frac{\text{fixed costs}}{\text{selling price per unit} - \text{variable cost per unit}} = \text{break-even}$$

c) Plot the **total costs line** on the chart below.

d) Plot the **total revenue line** on the chart below.

Break-Even Chart for Gnome Business

Costs and Revenues (£) vs Number of Gnomes Sold

Fixed costs

Break-Even Charts

Break-even charts show a business how much they need to sell to make a profit.

Profit and loss

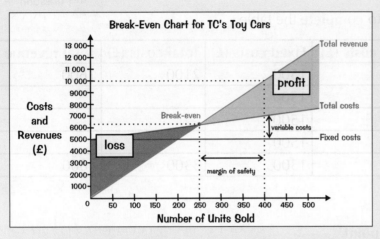

1) The space between the 'Total costs' and 'Total revenue' lines after the break-even point shows the profit-making area.

2) The space between the 'Total costs' and 'Total revenue' lines before the break-even point shows the loss-making area.

3) The gap between the 'Fixed costs' line and the 'Total costs' line shows the variable costs.

4) In this example, the business needs to sell 250 units to break even.

5) If the business sells more than 250 units, it will make a profit.

6) If it sells fewer than 250 units, it will make a loss.

Reminder
The **bigger** the **difference** between the target or actual sales and the break-even point, the **larger** the **margin of safety**.

Changes to variable costs

1) Changes to costs affect the break-even point.

2) If variable costs decrease, each unit costs less to produce.

3) This means a business needs to sell fewer units to break even.

4) If the variable costs increase, each unit costs more to produce.

5) This means a business has to sell more units to break even.

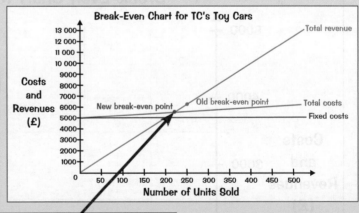

If the business's variable costs decrease to £2.50, the break-even point moves to the left of the chart. When costs increase, the break-even point moves to the right of the chart.

Practice Questions

1) True or false: the space between the 'Total costs' and 'Total revenue' lines before the break-even point shows the profit-making area.

2) What does the gap between the 'Fixed costs' line and the 'Total costs' line show?

Break-Even Charts

Changes in costs and sales price affect the break-even point.

If fixed costs increase

1) If fixed costs increase, the break-even point will be higher.
2) A higher break-even point means a business must sell more units to cover its costs.
3) If revenue stays the same, the business will make less profit.
4) If the costs are higher than the revenue, the business won't be able to break even, and they will make a loss.

If fixed costs decrease

1) If fixed costs decrease, the break-even point will be lower.
2) A lower break-even point means a business needs to sell fewer units to cover its costs.
3) If revenue stays the same, the business will make a larger profit.

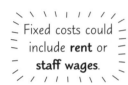

Fixed costs could include **rent** or **staff wages**.

If sales price increases

1) If a business increases the sales price of its products, the break-even point will be lower.
2) So the business needs to sell fewer units to cover its costs.
3) If the costs and total sales stay the same, the business will make a larger profit.
4) A business may increase the sales price if a product has become more expensive to make.
5) Sometimes businesses increase the sales price of their products to increase profits.

Sales price just means how much a customer pays for a product.

If sales price decreases

1) If a business decreases the sales price of a product, the break-even point will be higher.
2) So the business will need to sell more to cover its costs.
3) If the costs and total sales stay the same, the business will make less profit.
4) However, a lower price could attract more customers to buy a product, which could boost the total revenue.

Break-Even Chart Questions

Q1   Use the words below to **label** the break-even chart.

loss   margin of safety   variable costs   profit

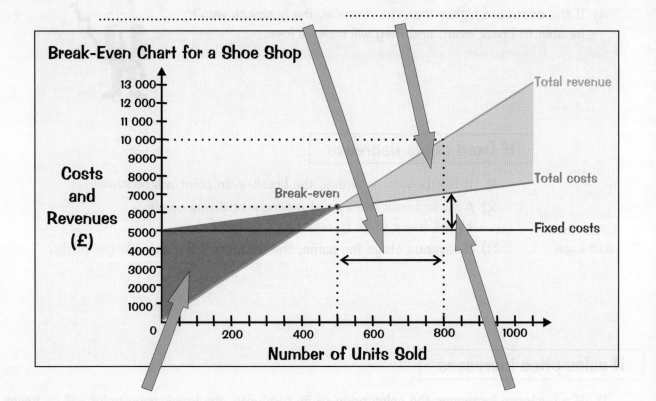

Break-Even Chart for a Shoe Shop

Costs and Revenues (£)

13 000, 12 000, 11 000, 10 000, 9000, 8000, 7000, 6000, 5000, 4000, 3000, 2000, 1000

Total revenue

Total costs

Break-even

Fixed costs

Number of Units Sold: 200, 400, 600, 800, 1000

Q2   Fill in the missing words in the sentences below.

loss   Total costs   profit

The space between the 'Total revenue' and 'Total costs' lines before the break-even point shows the .... -making area.

The space between the 'Total revenue' line and the 'Total costs' lines after the break-even point shows the .... -making area.

The variable costs are shown by the gap between the 'Fixed costs' and the '.................................' lines.

Break-Even Chart Questions

Q3 Are these sentences **true** or **false**? Tick the correct boxes.

                                                            True False

a) If the variable costs increase, the break-even point will be higher. ☐ ☐

b) If the fixed costs decrease, the break-even point will stay the same. ☐ ☐

c) If variable costs decrease, a business needs to sell fewer units to break even. ☐ ☐

d) When fixed costs increase, the break-even point will be higher. ☐ ☐

Q4 Match the boxes on the left with the correct box on the right.

| If the sales price increases... | ...the break-even point will increase. |

| If the sales price decreases... | ...the break-even point will decrease. |

Q5 Which of these is a possible **advantage** of a decrease in sales price? Tick **one** box.

a) The break-even point will be lower. ☐

b) The break-even point will be higher. ☐

c) More customers may be attracted to the product. ☐

Challenge Yourself
Q6

> Joseph sells car air-fresheners. His fixed costs are £1000 and his variable costs are £1 per air-freshener. He sells his products for £3 each. He calculates that his break-even point is 500 units.

a) Joseph's fixed costs increase to £1500. What will happen to his break-even point?

....

b) What does this mean for Joseph's sales?

....

Break-Even Analysis

Here are some of the benefits of analysing a break-even chart.

It can help a business set targets

1) Break-even analysis tells a business how many units it needs to sell to cover its costs.
2) It shows when a business will start to make a profit.
3) It shows the lowest number of sales needed to prevent a loss.
4) It can show a business the size of its margin of safety.
5) If the business's costs change it'll be able to predict how this will affect its profit or loss.

It can help a business adjust its costs and sales price

Break-even analysis can help a business decide how much it should sell its products for. It can also help a business decide whether its costs are too high.

Example 1

1) If a break-even point is very high, a business will have to sell a lot to make a profit.
2) Businesses could try to lower their break-even point to increase their profits.
3) They could do this by increasing the price of their products...
4) ...or decreasing their costs by using a cheaper supplier or cheaper materials.

Example 2

1) If a break-even point is low, a business can sell less and still make a profit.
2) So they might decide to reduce the sales price of their product to attract new customers and to beat the price of competitor products.
3) Or, they might decide to use the extra profit to expand or introduce a new product.

It can help new businesses plan for success

1) Break-even analysis can help persuade a bank to give a business a loan.
2) If a business can show it will start making a profit soon, it is more likely to convince a bank it will be a good investment.

Break-Even Analysis

There are quite a few risks if a business doesn't analyse a break-even chart.

Risks for planning

1) A business won't know how many products it has to sell before it starts making a profit.
2) It won't know the lowest amount of units it needs to sell to prevent a loss.
3) A business won't know its margin of safety.

Risks for pricing

1) A business won't know whether its products are priced too high or too low.
   - If the products are priced too low, the business will have to sell more to break even.
   - If it doesn't realise this, the business could risk making a loss.
2) If the sales price of the product changes, a business won't be able to predict what profit or loss it will make.

Risks for costs

1) A business won't know whether its costs are reasonable or not.
   - This could mean that more money is being spent on making the products and running the business than is being made by sales.
2) If the cost of making the product changes, a business won't be able to predict what profit or loss it will make.

Practice Questions

1) True or false: a break-even chart can show a business the size of its margin of safety.

2) True or false: if a break-even point increases, a business must sell less to make a profit.

3) True or false: if a break-even point is high, a business may try to find a cheaper supplier.

4) If the break-even point is low, would most businesses be more likely to increase or reduce their selling price?

Break-Even Analysis Questions

Q1 Are these sentences **true** or **false**? Tick the right boxes.

	True	False

a) Break-even analysis tells a business if customers will like a product. ☐ ☐

b) Break-even analysis tells a business how much it must sell to make a profit. ☐ ☐

c) Break-even analysis can be used to help prevent a business from making a loss. ☐ ☐

d) Break-even analysis shows if a bank will give a business a loan. ☐ ☐

Q2 Complete the sentences below using the words from the box.

units	business	increase	break-even

a) Break-even analysis helps a .... decide if a product's price is appropriate.

b) A business should realistically be able to meet its .... point.

c) A high break-even point suggests that a business will need to sell a lot of .... to make a profit.

d) A business might .... its sales price to lower the break-even point.

Q3 Which of the sentences below is the most likely reason for a business decreasing its prices? Tick **one** box.

☐ to sell fewer units

☐ to prevent a loss

☐ to attract more customers

☐ to persuade a bank to give it a loan

Q4 **Circle** the right words to complete these sentences.

a) A business can use break-even analysis to persuade **customers / a bank** to give them a loan.

b) This is especially important for **new / old** businesses.

c) A business can use a break-even chart to show that it is **a good investment / popular**.

Break-Even Analysis Questions

Q5 Which of the sentences below is **true**? Tick **one** box.

☐ A business could cut their fixed costs by using a more expensive supplier.

☐ To make more profit, a business might try to cut costs.

☐ If a business has a low break-even point, it will usually increase its sales price.

☐ Decreasing the sales price will cause a business to lose customers.

Q6 **Circle** the right words to complete these sentences.

a) Without break-even analysis, a business can't tell if its **costs / products** are reasonable or not.

b) It also means that it won't know the **most / least** it can sell without making a loss.

c) This could result in the business spending **more / less** money than it will make.

Q7 Which of these are **risks** that a business will face **without** a break-even analysis? Tick **two** boxes.

☐ It will be unable to make a profit.

☐ It will be unable to check if its target sales are achievable.

☐ It will not know when it will start making a profit.

☐ It will be unable to predict if customers will like a new product.

Challenge Yourself

Q8 Explain **two** reasons why a business should carry out a break-even analysis.

....

....

....

Budgeting

It's really important to budget the money going in and out of a business.

Budgets

1) Budgets predict or limit how much money a business is going to spend.
2) Budgets also predict how much money a business will receive.
3) Budgets also account for any money a business saves or borrows.

Expenditure budgets

1) An expenditure budget predicts how much money a business will spend over a period of time (usually a year).
2) It includes everything a business needs to spend money on, such as machinery, office rent and electricity.
3) Budgets can also set limits on spending to make sure that a business isn't overspending.

Example

Here's an expenditure budget for Dianne's DIY Supplies.

Expenditure (costs)	Budgeted cost (£)
wages	40 000
factory rent	10 000
stock	25 000
Total	75 000

Revenue budgets

1) A revenue budget predicts how much money will come into a business from sales (revenue) over a period of time.
2) A business will estimate how much it will sell, and the amount of money that it will receive from the total sales.
3) Businesses might use previous sales figures and market research to help them estimate how much they'll sell.

Example

Here's a revenue budget for Dianne's DIY Supplies.

Type of product	Budgeted revenue (£)
saw	50 000
hammer	34 000
other	26 000
Total	110 000

Planning ahead

1) Businesses have to think about anything that may affect their sales or spending when they make their budgets.
2) Advertising campaigns may cause both sales and spending to increase.
3) Competition from rival businesses might cause a drop in sales.

Budgeting

Make sure you understand the difference between budgeting and budgetary control.

Advantages of budgeting

1) Budgeting can prevent a business from spending more than it earns. If a business overspends, it could lose money and may go bankrupt.

2) Budgets can predict how much each department within a business will spend. So if a department is spending more than it should, managers know where in the business to try to reduce costs.

3) Managers can compare the budget to what was actually spent, and make improvements to next year's budget.

If a person or business is **bankrupt**, they have been declared by law as being unable to pay their debts.

Budgetary control

1) Budgetary control is when the budgeted figures are compared with the actual figures.

2) This means a business can compare its predicted performance with its actual performance.

3) If there is a difference between these figures, it is called a variance.

Example

Here's an example of budgetary control for Dianne's DIY Supplies.

What the business expected to make.

Month	Budgeted Revenue (£)	Actual Revenue (£)	Variance
January	130 000	131 000	1000
February	136 000	138 000	2000
March	142 000	138 000	(4000)

What the business actually made.

Figures in brackets have negative variance.

4) Budgetary control helps a business to work out why there is a variance.

5) If a business has more money than it budgeted, it could be because its advertising has been more successful, production is more effective, costs have decreased, or competitors are selling less.

6) If a business has less money than it budgeted, it could be because its advertising has been less successful, there are problems with production, costs have increased, or there's more competition from other businesses.

Practice Questions

1) True or false: an expenditure budget predicts how much a business will earn over a period of time.

2) What is the difference between budgeting and budgetary control?

Budgeting Questions

Q1   What is a **budget**? Tick the best definition.

☐ A list of things a business will spend money on.

☐ A plan of how much money will go in and out of a business.

☐ The amount of money a business can spend while still making a profit.

☐ The break-even point minus the margin of safety.

Q2   Circle **three** words from the boxes below which might be shown on an **expenditure budget**.

revenue   office rent   profit from shares   stock   staff wages

Q3   Complete the sentences below. Use the words from the box.

market research   advertising campaign   revenue

A .... budget predicts how much

money a business will receive over a period of time. A business can make these

predictions using .... and previous sales

figures. A good .... should increase sales.

Q4   Choose whether these sentences about **budgeting** are **true** or **false**.

	True	False
a) Budgeting can prevent a business from spending more than it earns.	☐	☐
b) Limits can be set in a budget to limit a business's revenue.	☐	☐
c) Budgeting means that a business is aware of how much it should be spending.	☐	☐
d) If a business doesn't stay within its budget, it could become bankrupt.	☐	☐

Budgeting Questions

Q5 Match the beginning of each sentence with the correct ending on the right.

A business may end up with more money than budgeted...

...if costs increase.

Budgetary control is...

...when there is a difference between the actual figures and budgeted figures.

Variance is...

...if better advertising is used.

A business may have less money than expected...

...when budgeted figures are compared with the actual figures.

Challenge Yourself

Q6 Complete this budgetary control table for Kate's café by filling in the **variance** column for February and March.

Month	Budgeted Revenue (£)	Actual Revenue (£)	Variance
January	10 000	9000	(1000)
February	12 000	13 000	
March	12 000	11 000	

Q7 Which of the following is the most likely reason for the café's negative variance in January. Tick **one** box.

☐ supplier problems

☐ more effective marketing

☐ decreased competitor activity

Cash Flow Forecasting

Cash flow forecasts are another way a business can keep an eye on its money.

Cash flow forecasts

1) A cash flow forecast identifies all the money that will be coming in (inflows) and going out (outflows) of a business over a period of time.

2) It is a way of predicting if a business will have enough money to pay its debts.

3) The forecast should be updated if there are any unexpected cash inflows or outflows so that the business can predict any problems.

Cash inflows

1) Cash inflows include all the money that a business receives.

Inflow examples

- Sale of products
- Interest on savings
- Sale of assets, such as old machinery
- Borrowed money, such as loans

Businesses sometimes invest money in high interest bank accounts to make more money. See p.10.

2) Inflows can be regular or irregular:
- Regular inflows are money that a business receives on a regular basis, such as monthly sales or annual interest.
- Irregular inflows, like loans or the sale of assets, don't happen all the time.

Cash outflows

1) 'Cash outflows' is another way of saying 'all the money that leaves a business'.

Outflow examples

- Payments for stock or raw materials
- Wages and bills
- Payments for equipment
- Loan repayments

2) Cash outflows can be regular or irregular:
- Regular outflows (wages, bills, loan repayments and buying stock) can be predicted.
- Irregular outflows, like repairs or new equipment, are harder to predict.

3) Businesses should set money aside for irregular outflows when making a cash flow forecast to avoid any cash flow problems.

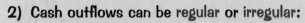

Cash Flow Forecasting

Example

Here's a cash flow forecast for Chip's Chocolate Business.

The total outflow is all the money which leaves the business.

The total inflow is all the money which comes into the business.

'-' before the number shows that it is a negative number.

Net cash flow is the total inflow minus the total outflow. If the outflow is bigger than the inflow, the net cash flow will be negative.

	December	January	February	March
Total inflow (£)	14 000	3000	7000	12 000
Total outflow (£)	11 000	8000	8500	9000
Net cash flow (£)	3000	-5000	-1500	3000
Opening bank balance (£)	1000	4000	-1000	-2500
Closing bank balance (£)	4000	-1000	-2500	500

Work out the closing bank balance at the end of each month by adding the net cash flow to the opening balance.

Improving cash flow

All businesses need to have enough money to cover the cost of their outflows.
Here are some ways a business might try to improve its cash flow:

Encourage customers to pay with cash. → If customers pay with cash, the business will receive the money more quickly than if they pay by cheque or credit card.

Encourage customers to pay straight away. → If customers aren't given a credit period, the business will receive its money sooner, so it will have cash to cover its costs.

Get a credit period with suppliers. → Having a credit period with suppliers means that a business will have time to receive payment from customers before it needs to pay its suppliers. See p.44 for more on credit periods.

Sell extra stock. → Most firms keep a stock of unsold products. Rather than buying more stock, it could focus on selling the extra stock.

But this is only a short-term solution. Eventually the business will run out of products and will have to start paying out money to buy more stock.

Practice Question

1) Give two examples of cash inflows.

Section Two — Planning for Success

Analysing Cash Flow

These pages will help you understand what a cash flow forecast tells you about a business.

Cash flow

1) Cash flow forecasts tell you when a business might not have enough money to cover its outflows. This is called a 'deficit'.

2) They can also tell you when a business might have extra money in their account. This is called a 'surplus'.

Cash deficit

1) A cash flow forecast can be used to predict when a business will have negative cash flow, or a deficit.

Example

Here is a cash flow forecast for Minnie's cheese shop.

	January	February	March	April
Sales revenue	25 000	20 000	30 000	25 000
Other inflows				
Total inflow (£)	25 000	20 000	30 000	25 000
Wages and rent	20 000	20 000	20 000	20 000
Other outflows		25 000		
Total outflow (£)	20 000	45 000	20 000	20 000
Net cash flow (£)	5000	-25 000	10 000	5000
Opening bank balance (£)	10 000	15 000	-10 000	0
Closing bank balance (£)	15 000	-10 000	0	5000

Other outflows could be things like advertising, machinery, or a staff training programme.

Minnie will have a cash deficit at the end of February.

2) The £25 000 of other outflows in February means that Minnie will be left with a negative closing bank balance (or deficit) at the end of the month (-£10 000).

3) To prevent this, Minnie could arrange a loan at the end of January to cover the extra outflows.

4) Or she could try to spread the extra outflows over a longer period of time, so that they cause fewer problems.

Analysing Cash Flow

Cash surplus

1) A cash flow forecast can predict when a business will have a cash surplus.

2) A business should have enough money to cover its outflows, and a bit extra in case of any unexpected costs.

This business tries to keep £5000 to one side for unexpected costs — any money left over after this is a surplus. This cash flow forecast shows that the business will have a cash surplus during September to December.

	September	October	November	December
Sales revenue	25 000	30 000	30 000	35 000
Other inflows		5000		
Total inflow (£)	25 000	35 000	30 000	35 000
Wages and rent	20 000	20 000	20 000	30 000
Other outflows				
Total outflow (£)	20 000	20 000	20 000	30 000
Net cash flow (£)	5000	15 000	10 000	5000
Opening bank balance (£)	10 000	15 000	30 000	40 000
Closing bank balance (£)	15 000	30 000	40 000	45 000

3) A business could use a cash surplus to make even more profit.

4) It could move some of the money into a high interest savings account.

5) Or the money could be reinvested into the business.

Examples of reinvestment

- Introduce a new product or service
- Produce more of existing products
- Extra advertising
- Invest in new resources such as machinery
- Open a new premises, such as a new office, shop or café
- Invest in staff training

Different times of year

1) Certain products sell better at specific times of year. These are called seasonal products.

2) For example, calendars sell well between November and January, but rarely sell at other times.

3) Cash flow forecasts help to predict whether seasonal products will make enough profit during the busy months to make up for the quieter months.

Practice Questions

1) What does cash deficit mean?

2) What does cash surplus mean?

Cash Flow Forecasting Questions

Q1   What is a **cash flow forecast**? Tick the best definition.

☐   A prediction of all the money going in and out of a business over a period of time.

☐   A prediction of what the break-even point will be.

☐   A prediction of what the budgetary control will show at the end of the year.

Q2   Match each term with the correct **definition**.

One has been done for you.

Outflow

Inflow

Closing bank balance

Net cash flow

inflow minus the outflow

money going out of a business

money going into a business

opening bank balance plus the net cash flow

Q3   Choose whether these sentences are **true** or **false**.

		True	False
a)	Monthly sales are a regular inflow for a business.	☐	☐
b)	Sales of assets are a regular inflow for a business.	☐	☐
c)	Irregular outflows are easier to predict than regular outflows.	☐	☐

Q4   What could a business do to **improve** its **cash flow**? Circle **two** boxes.

Ask customers to pay with 3 months' credit.

Ask customers to pay by cash.

Arrange a credit period with its suppliers.

Pay its bills late.

Analysing Cash Flow Questions

Q1 What could a business do if they predict that they will have a cash **deficit**?
Tick **one** box.

☐ Invest in new resources.

☐ Launch a new advertising campaign.

☐ Arrange a short-term loan.

Q2 What might a business do if they predict that they will have a cash **surplus**?
Tick **one** box.

☐ Try to spread its costs over a longer period of time.

☐ Invest in new resources.

☐ Organise an overdraft for the business account.

Challenge Yourself

Q3 a) Complete this **cash flow forecast**.

You can use a calculator for this question.

$$\text{Net cash flow} = \text{total inflow} - \text{total outflow}$$

$$\text{Closing bank balance} = \text{opening bank balance} + \text{net cash flow}$$

	January	February	March
Total inflow (£)	5000	5000	4000
Total outflow (£)	2000	2000	3000
Net cash flow (£)			
Opening bank balance (£)	1000		
Closing bank balance (£)			

b) Using the cash flow forecast, suggest what action the business could take to manage its finances over this period.

....

....

....

Timings and Cash Flow Forecasting

The timings of payments into, and out of, a business can affect the cash flow forecast.

Timings of inflows and outflows

1) There is often a delay between a business's outflows and their inflows.

2) Sometimes customers are given a credit period before they have to pay.

3) This means that the business doesn't receive the money straightaway.

4) Businesses need to think about these timings when creating a cash flow forecast.

Example — Instant payment

1) Chip's Chocolate Business has just opened. This cash flow forecast predicts that customers will pay for the products straightaway.

This business is new, so their 'Opening bank balance' is their start-up capital.

	December	January	February	March
Total inflow (£)	14 000	3000	7000	12 000
Total outflow (£)	11 000	8000	8500	9000
Net cash flow (£)	3000	-5000	-1500	3000
Opening bank balance (£)	3000	6000	1000	-500
Closing bank balance (£)	6000	1000	-500	2500

2) In January and February, Chip's outflow will be bigger than his inflow.

3) This will result in a negative net cash flow.

4) Chip will need to take action to improve this negative cash flow, perhaps by organising an overdraft or short-term loan for February.

Example — One month credit period

1) If customers have one month's credit, the business's monthly inflow and bank balance will change. This might affect if and when a loan is needed.

2) This is the same cash flow forecast as above, but the customers have a one month credit period.

There will be no inflow in December because it is a new business, and with the month's credit period, there won't be any money flowing in for the first month of business.

The payment for the total sales isn't received by the business until one month later.

	December	January	February	March
Total sales this month (for payment in 1 month)	14 000	3000	7000	12 000
Total inflow (£)	0	14 000	3000	7000
Total outflow (£)	11 000	8000	8500	9000
Net cash flow (£)	-11 000	6000	-5500	-2000
Opening bank balance (£)	3000	-8000	-2000	-7500
Closing bank balance (£)	-8000	-2000	-7500	-9500

3) On this new forecast, action needs to be taken straightaway in December.

The Importance of Cash Flow Forecasts

Advantages of cash flow forecasts

Businesses create cash flow forecasts to predict problems and plan ahead.

Predicting problems

1) A cash flow forecast identifies whether a business will have a cash deficit.

2) It predicts if funds will be low, so that a business has enough time to arrange a loan or overdraft, or reduce its outflows.

3) It can identify if a business will have long-term cash flow problems.

Planning for success

1) A cash flow forecast can also predict if there will be a cash surplus.

2) This extra money can be used to make the business even more profitable.

3) The money could be reinvested in the business or in a high-interest savings account.

Decision-making

1) A cash flow forecast can identify whether a new business has raised enough start-up capital.

2) Cash flow forecasts make it easier for businesses to make difficult decisions. For example, they can predict when they will have enough money to buy new equipment.

Risks of not completing a cash flow forecast

1) Without a cash flow forecast, a business can't tell if it will be able to pay its bills.

2) This means a business won't know to arrange a loan or reduce its outflows.

3) If a business can't pay its suppliers on time, the suppliers might not deliver the products.

4) This could stop production and could lead to bankruptcy.

Practice Questions

1) True or false: if customers have a two month credit period, they have two months to pay for their product.

2) Give one example of a problem that a cash flow forecast could predict.

Timings and Cash Flow Forecasting Questions

Q1 Complete the sentences below. Use the words from the box.

credit	delay	selling	timings	survive

A business must manage the .... of its inflows and outflows in

order to .... Sometimes, there is a .... between

the business .... a product and the customer paying for it. This is

because customers are given a .... period before they have to pay.

Q2 This cash flow forecast assumes that this new business will be paid **instantly**.

	January	February	March	April
Total inflow (£)	4000	3000	5000	11 000
Total outflow (£)	1000	8000	6000	4000
Net cash flow (£)	3000	-5000	-1000	7000
Opening bank balance (£)	500	3500	-1500	-2500
Closing bank balance (£)	3500	-1500	-2500	4500

a) Which of these actions could the business take by February
to improve its financial position? Tick **one** box.

☐ Invest its cash surplus in a new product

☐ Organise a loan

☐ Buy new equipment

This cash flow forecast assumes that customers will pay after **one month**.

	January	February	March	April	May
Total inflow (£)	0	4000	3000	5000	11 000
Total outflow (£)	1000	8000	6000	4000	2000
Net cash flow (£)	-1000	-4000	-3000	1000	9000
Opening bank balance (£)	500	-500	-4500	-7500	-6500
Closing bank balance (£)	-500	-4500	-7500	-6500	2500

b) How will the business's action, from **part a)**, be different now?

....

The Importance of Cash Flow Forecasts Questions

Q1   **Circle** the right words to complete the sentences.

a) Cash flow forecasts can help a business predict when they will have low funds / resources.

b) This means that it could arrange advertising / loans for these periods.

c) It can also prove to a bank that a business will be able to spend / repay any loans.

d) A cash flow forecast shouldn't / should be updated if there are unexpected inflows.

Q2   Complete the sentences below. Use the words from the box.

| money   decisions   surplus   machinery   capital |

Cash flow forecasts make it easier for managers to make ....
such as when to launch a new product or buy new ....
A cash flow forecast shows whether a new business has enough start-up
.... It also shows if the business will have enough
.... to pay its staff and bills.
Cash flow forecasts can also predict if a business will have a cash
................................, so they can plan how to use this money to make the
business more profitable.

Q3   Are these sentences **true** or **false**? Tick the right boxes.
        Without a cash flow forecast...   **True** **False**

a) ... a business can't tell if it will be able to pay its bills.   ☐   ☐

b) ... a business will have a cash deficit.   ☐   ☐

c) ... a business can't get a loan.   ☐   ☐

d) ... a business won't be prepared for times of low income.   ☐   ☐

Creating a Cash Flow Forecast

You might be asked to complete a cash flow forecast in the exam, so read through these pages so you'll know what you're doing.

Creating a cash flow forecast

Here's an example of how to create a cash flow forecast.

Example

1) At Terry's Tangerine Shop customers are given one month's credit.
2) In February, he sold £500 of tangerines.
3) He will receive a loan of £2000 in March.
4) He expects to sell:
   - £1000 of tangerines in March
   - £2000 of tangerines in April
   - £3000 of tangerines in May
   - £4000 of tangerines in June
5) He pays £1500 a month for staff wages and rent.
6) The cost of equipment varies throughout the year:
   - £200 in March
   - £400 in April
   - £400 in May
   - £500 in June
7) Terry's closing balance at the end of February was £1000.

Reminder
If customers have a 'month's credit', the sales should be included in the 'inflows' for the **next month**.

Step one — inflows

1) Terry's regular inflows are his sales revenue.
2) His customers do not have to pay straightaway, so the revenue for each month will be received the following month.
3) He receives a loan of £2000 in March.

Inflows might also be called 'receipts'.

The £500 worth of tangerines sold in February are the sales revenue for March.

	March	April	May	June
Total sales this month (for payment in 1 month)	1000	2000	3000	4000
Sales revenue	500	1000	2000	3000
Other inflows	2000			
Total inflow (£)	2500	1000	2000	3000

Other inflows could include loans, grants, start-up capital and sales of land or machinery.

Section Two — Planning for Success

Creating a Cash Flow Forecast

Step two — outflows

1) Terry's employees' wages and rent are regular outflows adding up to £1500 a month.

2) The cost of equipment changes each month, but it is still a regular outflow.

	March	April	May	June
Sales revenue	500	1000	2000	3000
Other inflows	2000			
Total inflow (£)	2500	1000	2000	3000
Wages and Rent	1500	1500	1500	1500
Equipment	200	400	400	500
Total Outflow (£)	1700	1900	1900	2000

Outflows might also be called 'payments'.

Other examples of outflows could include advertising, stock, raw materials or bills.

Step three — net cash flow and bank balances

1) The net cash flow for a month is the difference between the total inflow and the total outflow for that month.

2) The opening bank balance for the month is the closing balance for the month before.

3) The closing bank balance is the opening bank balance plus the net cash flow.

Reminder
When you're adding a negative number you must subtract it. For example, $50 + -20 = 50 - 20$.

	March	April	May	June
Sales revenue	500	1000	2000	3000
Other inflows	2000			
Total inflow (£)	2500	1000	2000	3000
Wages and Rent	1500	1500	1500	1500
Equipment	200	400	400	500
Total Outflow (£)	1700	1900	1900	2000
Net Cash Flow	800	-900	100	1000
Opening Bank Balance	1000	1800	900	1000
Closing Bank Balance	1800	900	1000	2000

Here, the net cash flow for April is -900 (1000 minus 1900).

The closing bank balance for April is the opening bank balance (1800) plus the net cash flow (-900), which is 900.

The opening bank balance for April is 1800 because it's the same as the closing bank balance for March.

Practice Question

1) True or false: net cash flow is all the inflows for a given month added together.

Creating a Cash Flow Forecast Questions

Q1 Use the information in the box to complete the **inflows** for the cash flow forecast below.

> Rhiannon sells BBQs. Her customers are given one month's credit and all pay one month after their purchase. She has a loan of £100 in June. In May she sold £300 of BBQs, and she has predicted her sales figures for the next 3 months:
>
> June: £700
>
> July: £600
>
> August: £600

	June	July	August	September
Sales revenue (£)	300			
Other inflows (£)	100	0	0	0
Total inflow (£)	400			

sales revenue + other inflows = total inflow

Q2 Complete this cash flow forecast by working out the **net cash flow**, **opening bank balances** and **closing bank balances**.

	January	February	March	April
Sales revenue	1000	1000	4000	5000
Other inflows	-	-	-	-
Total inflow (£)	1000	1000	4000	5000
Wages and rent	2000	3000	2000	2000
Total outflow (£)	2000	3000	2000	2000
Net cash flow				
Opening bank balance	2000			
Closing bank balance				

total inflow − total outflow = net cash flow

net cash flow + opening bank balance = closing bank balance

Q3 Using the **cash flow forecast** from Q2, decide whether these sentences are **true** or **false**.

	True	False
a) The business will need a short-term loan for February.	☐	☐
b) At the end of March, the business will have a negative closing bank balance.	☐	☐
c) The business will need a short-term loan at the end of April.	☐	☐

Creating a Cash Flow Forecast Questions

Q4 Miranda owns a market stall. She has made a **cash flow forecast** for four months:

	January	February	March	April
Sales revenue	100	200	200	300
Other inflows	-	-	300	-
Total inflow	100	200	500	300
Wages and rent	200	200	200	200
Other outflows	-	-	100	-
Total outflow	200	200	300	200
Net cash flow	-100	0	200	100
Opening bank balance	200	100	100	300
Closing bank balance	100	100	300	400

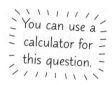

You can use a calculator for this question.

a) She has forgotten to include an **extra outflow** of £400 for **February**.
Complete this new cash flow forecast for the market stall using this information.

	January	February	March	April
Sales revenue	100	200	200	300
Other inflows	-	-	300	-
Total inflow	100	200	500	300
Wages and rent	200	200	200	200
Other outflows	-		100	-
Total outflow	200		300	200
Net cash flow	-100		200	100
Opening bank balance	200			
Closing bank balance	100			

b) Which of these are possible reasons for this extra **outflow**? Tick **one** box.

☐ A bank loan

☐ An advertising campaign

☐ The sale of assets

c) Looking at the new cash flow forecast, what **action** must Miranda now take?

....

Gross and Net Profit

You need to know how to calculate gross profit. It's all here on a page for you.

Cost of sales

1) Cost of sales is the cost of producing a product.
2) It is the total of all the direct costs (see p.6), like stock, raw materials and labour.

Gross profit

1) Gross profit is the money left once the cost of sales is taken away from the revenue.
2) Gross profit tells you how much money a business has made before expenses like salaries and rent are taken away.
3) Gross profit can be either positive or negative.

> **Reminder**
> Revenue is all the money a business receives.

Calculating gross profit

Here's the formula for working out gross profit:

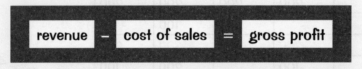

revenue − cost of sales = gross profit

> You won't be given the gross profit formula in the exam, so make sure you learn it.

Example

JMA Games makes computer games. Their revenue for 2012 was £525 000 and their cost of sales was £390 455. Calculate their gross profit for 2012.

revenue   £525 000 − £390 455   = £134 545

cost of sales   positive gross profit

Positive and negative gross profit

1) The larger the gross profit, the greater the chance of a positive net profit (see p.53).
2) Positive gross profit doesn't always mean that net profit will be positive.
3) If the gross profit is negative, there is nothing left to deduct overheads from. This means there will be no chance of the business making a net profit.

Gross and Net Profit

Now you know about gross profit, it's time to get down to the nitty-gritty... net profit.

Net profit

1) Net profit is the money left over once all costs have been deducted.
2) To make net profit, gross profit needs to be positive.

Calculating net profit

Use this formula to work out net profit:

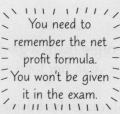

You need to remember the net profit formula. You won't be given it in the exam.

$$\boxed{\text{gross profit}} - \boxed{\text{expenditure}} = \boxed{\text{net profit}}$$

Example

Pink Pizzas sells takeaway pizzas. Their gross profit for 2010 was £39 000 and their expenditure was £48 225. Calculate their net profit for 2010.

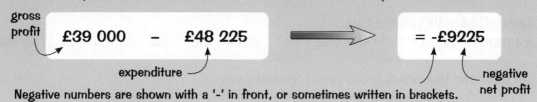

gross profit → £39 000   –   £48 225   ⟹   = -£9225

expenditure

negative net profit

Negative numbers are shown with a '-' in front, or sometimes written in brackets.

Positive and negative net profit

1) If a business has a positive net profit, it is making a profit.
2) The business could use this profit to expand the business, invest in high interest savings accounts, pay shareholders or put some money aside for unexpected costs.
3) If the net profit is negative, the business is said to be operating at a loss.

Practice Questions

1) True or false: you need to know the cost of sales to work out the gross profit.
2) True or false: positive gross profit always results in a positive net profit.
3) True or false: if gross profit is negative, a business is operating at a loss.
4) Give one example of what a business can do with its money if its net profit is positive.

Gross and Net Profit Questions

Q1 Complete the formula for **gross profit**. Use words from the box.

| expenditure | revenue | cost of sales | net profit |

.... – .... = **gross profit**

Q2 a) Georgie owns a gardening business.
Last year, her total **revenue** was **£25 000** and her **cost of sales** was **£18 500**.

Calculate the business's **gross profit** for last year.

Gross profit = | £

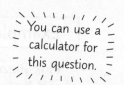
You can use a calculator for this question.

b) Classic-Cars sells vintage cars.
Last month, their **cost of sales** was **£107 500** and their total **revenue** was **£106 000**.

Calculate the business's **gross profit** for last year.

Gross profit = | £

c) From your answer to part **b)**, say whether Classic-Cars was **financially successful** or **unsuccessful** last year. Give a reason for your answer.

....

Q3 Circle the right words in the sentences below.

Net / Gross profit is the money a business has left over after all its costs have been taken away.

Net / Gross profit is the money a business has left over once the cost of sales has been taken away.

Gross and Net Profit Questions

Q4   Complete the formula for **net profit**. Use words from the box.

> expenditure   variable costs   gross profit   revenue

> .... – .... = net profit

Q5 a) Sam owns a camera shop.
Last year, his **gross profit** was **£11 000**, and his **expenditure** was **£9500**.

Calculate the business's **net profit** for last year.

Net profit = £

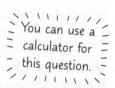
You can use a calculator for this question.

b) Imogen runs a translation business.
Her **expenditure** last year was **£3750**, and her **gross profit** was **£5000**.

Calculate how much **net profit** Imogen made last year.

Net profit = £

Challenge Yourself

Q6   Tom owns a construction business.
Here is some of his financial information from last year:

You can use a calculator for this question.

- total revenue — **£54 000**

- cost of sales — **£35 000**

- expenditure — **£10 000**

a) Calculate how much **gross profit** Tom made last year.

Gross profit = £

b) Calculate how much **net profit** Tom made last year.

Net profit = £

Income Statements

There are a couple of ways a business can record how it's doing. Read on to find out about them.

Financial statements

1) Businesses can measure their success with financial statements.
2) Financial statements record what a business is doing with its money.
3) Sometimes businesses have to keep financial statements by law.
4) Two types of financial statement are:
   - an income statement (also known as a profit and loss account)
   - a statement of financial position (also known as a balance sheet)

Income statement (profit and loss account)

Income statements show how much money a business has made, usually over a year.

This top part is called the trading account. It records a business's gross profit.

'Sales' is another way of saying 'revenue'. It might also be written as 'turnover'.

A business has to buy raw materials to make its products or buy stock from manufacturers. These come under purchases.

Reminder

revenue − cost of sales = gross profit

This bottom part lists all of the business's expenditure (expenses and overheads). This is taken away from the gross profit to work out the net profit.

Example

Trading, Profit and Loss Account
Super Sport Shop Ltd.
Year ending 31st March 2012

	£000	£000
Sales		650
Cost of sales:		
Opening stock	52	
Purchases	98	
	150	
Minus closing stock	41	
Cost of sales =		109
Gross profit =		541
Minus expenses:		
Wages and salaries	95	
Rent and rates	8	
Office expenses	18	
Advertising	12	
Depreciation	5	
Other expenses	2	
Total expenses =		140
Net profit =		401

Many established firms start the year with leftover stock from the previous year. This is opening stock.

This figure is opening stock added to purchases.

Closing stock is calculated by adding up the value of all the goods not yet sold.

Reminder

gross profit − expenditure = net profit

Income Statements

You might need to complete an income statement in the exam. It can be quite fiddly, so make sure you read all the figures carefully and take your time. Here's a worked exam question.

Filling in an income statement

- The items below need to be entered into the income statement (profit and loss account) for Snazzy Stationery Ltd.

Income from sales £74 200	Cost of sales £22 125	Wages and salaries £20 990	Rent and rates £12 500

- Write your answers in the white boxes in the table.
- Some information has already been entered.

Income from sales is another way of saying revenue or turnover.

Income from sales always goes at the top.

You need to work out gross profit yourself.

These are both types of expense, so they go under expenses.

Reminder
$$\text{revenue} - \text{cost of sales} = \text{gross profit}$$

	£	£
Income from sales		74 200
Cost of sales	22 125	
Gross Profit		52 075
Expenses		
Wages and salaries	20 990	
Rent and rates	12 500	
Total expenses	33 490	
Net profit		18 585

Work this out yourself by adding up the expenses.

To work out the net profit, take the total expenses (expenditure) away from the gross profit.

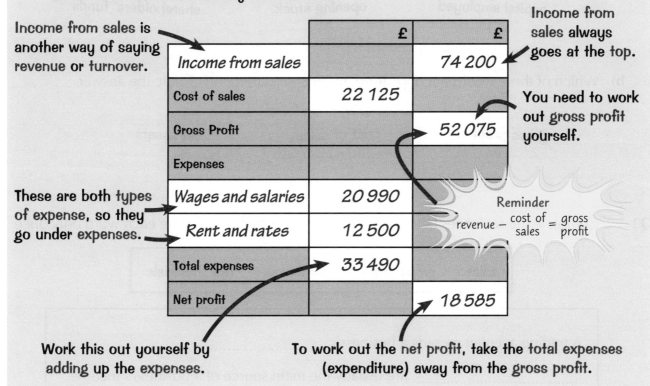

Practice Questions

1) True or false: financial statements help a business measure its success.

2) Where would you find net profit on an income statement — in the top or bottom section?

3) Does a trading account record gross profit or net profit?

4) True or false: gross profit is found in the bottom part of an income statement.

5) True or false: income statements show how much revenue a business has made.

Income Statement Questions

Q1   Circle the right words in the sentences below.

An income statement is also known as a **profit and loss account** / balance sheet.

Net profit is usually a **smaller** / larger number than gross profit.

A trading account goes at the bottom / **top** of an income statement.

Q2 a)   Which of these might appear on an **income statement**? Circle the answer.

capital employed   opening stock   shareholders' funds

b)   Which of these would **not** appear on an **income statement**? Circle the answer.

gross profit   cost of sales   net assets

Q3   Complete the sentences below. Use the words from the box. Use each word only once.

sales   gross profit   purchases   raw materials

A trading account records a business's ....

.... are usually the main source of a business's income.

To generate sales, a business has to spend money on things like

...., which come under ....

on an income statement.

Q4   Circle the right words in the sentences below.

Cost of sales / Rent is found under expenses on an income statement.

Opening stock / Closing stock is all the stock left over from the previous year.

Income Statement Questions

Q5 Read each sentence below and then circle true or false.

a) Income statements are usually based on financial information over two years. **true / false**

b) Net profit is calculated in the bottom part of an income statement. **true / false**

c) 'Revenue' is another word for 'cost of sales'. **true / false**

Challenge Yourself

Q6 The items below need to be entered into the income statement (profit and loss account) for RJ's Travel Business Ltd.

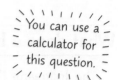
You can use a calculator for this question.

Income from sales £54 300	Cost of sales £15 600	Advertising £1200	Office expenses £1050

Write your answers in the gaps in the table. Some information has already been entered.

	£	£
....		....
Cost of sales	....	
Gross Profit		....
Expenses		
....	....	
....	....	
Total expenses	....	
Net profit		....

Statements of Financial Position

Statements of financial position record where a business got its money from. They're also known as balance sheets.

Statement of financial position (balance sheet)

1) A balance sheet helps businesses to:
   - Know how much they're worth.
   - Know what they own and what they owe to other people.
2) A balance sheet is only valid for the day it is written.

What does a balance sheet show?

The following things are shown on a business's balance sheet:
1) assets — what the business owns and what is owed to it.
2) liabilities — what the business owes to other people or other businesses.
3) capital — how the business is funded.

Assets

1) Assets are normally the first thing on a balance sheet.
2) There are two types of assets: fixed assets and current assets.

Fixed assets

1) Fixed assets are things like buildings and machinery that can't be turned into cash easily.
2) They can be shown on a balance sheet as their 'cost' price (the price that was originally paid for them), or as their 'net value' price (their 'cost' price with any depreciation deducted).

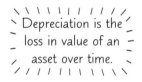

Depreciation is the loss in value of an asset over time.

Current assets (short-term assets)

1) Current assets are things like money owed to the business (also known as trade receivables or debtors), cash and stock.
2) The value of current assets changes all the time.
3) For example, a business's stock levels go up and down depending on sales and production.
4) Current assets are known as liquid assets. This means that they can be sold quickly.
5) On a balance sheet, current assets are shown in the reverse order of liquidity.
6) This means the least liquid asset comes first, for example stock. The most liquid asset (usually cash) comes last.

The more liquid something is, the easier it is to turn it into cash.

Statements of Financial Position

Liabilities

1) Liabilities are what a business owes to others.
2) They can be categorised as current liabilities or long-term liabilities.

Current liabilities

1) Current liabilities are short-term debts that must be paid off quickly (within a year).
2) A creditor (someone the business owes money to) is an example of a current liability.
3) The business's supplier could be a creditor. A business might owe money for purchases it has made on credit (trade payables).
4) The value of current liabilities is always changing (or liquid).
5) Current liabilities are usually found in the top section of a balance sheet, after fixed and current assets (see p.63 for an example of a balance sheet).

Long-term liabilities

1) Long-term liabilities usually take over a year to pay off.
2) Examples include things like bank loans or mortgages.
3) Long-term liabilities are usually found in the external capital section of a balance sheet because they show how a business has been funded.

Capital

1) The capital section of a balance sheet shows where the business got its money from.
2) Capital can be split into two main sources:
   - Internal — Internal capital is money raised from within the business. Examples of internal capital are share capital (when shareholders invest money into the business) and profit that has been reinvested into the business.
   - External — External capital is money that has been borrowed from outside the business and must be repaid. A bank loan is an example of external capital.

Practice Questions

1) True or false: depreciation is the gain in value of an asset over time.
2) True or false: liabilities are what a business owes to others.
3) Give one example of a current asset.
4) Give one example of internal capital.

Statements of Financial Position

Once you've worked out a business's assets, liabilities and sources of capital, you can use those figures to help you work out its working capital, net assets and capital employed.

Working capital (net current assets)

1) Working capital might also be called net current assets. They're the same thing.

2) Working capital is the money that's available to pay for the day-to-day running of the business, like staff wages or bills.

3) This is the formula for working capital:

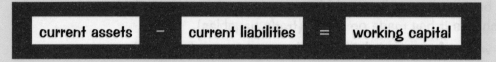

current assets   —   current liabilities   =   working capital

4) If working capital is too low or negative, the business may have problems paying for its day-to-day activities.

5) If it's too high, money isn't being used efficiently and there might be wasted opportunities for investing the money elsewhere in the business.

6) Working capital should be enough to cover costs with a little left over for emergencies.

Net assets

1) The figure for net assets shows the money the business would make if it sold all its assets. It's what the business is worth.

2) To work out net assets, you need to calculate working capital first.

3) This is the formula for working out net assets:

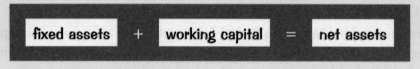

fixed assets   +   working capital   =   net assets

Capital employed

1) A balance sheet will usually give a figure for capital employed.

2) Capital employed shows how much money has been invested into the business.

3) To work out the capital employed, add all the sources of capital together, including the long-term liabilities.

4) The figure for capital employed and the figure for net assets should be the same.

5) This is because capital employed shows how the business is funded, and net assets shows how the business is using those funds.

Statements of Financial Position

Here's an example of a balance sheet. It looks complicated, but if you go through it one step at a time, it won't be as bad as it seems...

Balance sheet

Balance sheets show what a business owes and owns on a given date.

Not all balance sheets look the same. Don't be confused if you see one that looks different.

Example

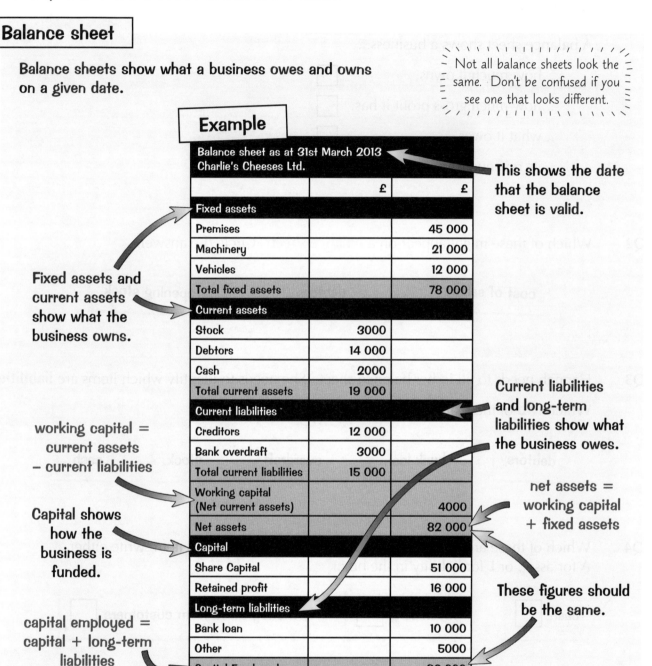

Balance sheet as at 31st March 2013
Charlie's Cheeses Ltd.

	£	£
Fixed assets		
Premises		45 000
Machinery		21 000
Vehicles		12 000
Total fixed assets		78 000
Current assets		
Stock	3000	
Debtors	14 000	
Cash	2000	
Total current assets	19 000	
Current liabilities		
Creditors	12 000	
Bank overdraft	3000	
Total current liabilities	15 000	
Working capital (Net current assets)		4000
Net assets		82 000
Capital		
Share Capital		51 000
Retained profit		16 000
Long-term liabilities		
Bank loan		10 000
Other		5000
Capital Employed		82 000

This shows the date that the balance sheet is valid.

Fixed assets and current assets show what the business owns.

Current liabilities and long-term liabilities show what the business owes.

working capital = current assets – current liabilities

net assets = working capital + fixed assets

Capital shows how the business is funded.

capital employed = capital + long-term liabilities

These figures should be the same.

Practice Questions

1) True or false: a balance sheet is valid for 12 months after it has been written.

2) True or false: the capital section of a balance sheet shows how the business is funded.

3) What is working capital also known as?

Statement of Financial Position Questions

Q1 What does a **balance sheet** show a business?
Tick two boxes.

A balance sheet shows a business...

...how much it owns. ☐

...how much gross profit it has. ☐

...what it owes. ☐

...its revenue from sales. ☐

Q2 Which of these might appear on a **balance sheet**? Circle the answer.

cost of sales   debtors   opening stock

Q3 Hannah needs to fill in her balance sheet. She needs to identify which items are **liabilities**.

Which **two** of these are **liabilities**? Circle **two** boxes.

debtors   bank loan   overdraft   stock   cash

Q4 Which of these are **assets** and which are **liabilities**? For each item, write either
A for asset, or **L** for liability in the box.

cash ☐   machinery ☐   money owed from customers ☐

money owed to suppliers ☐   mortgage payments ☐   stock ☐

Q5 What is **working capital**? Tick the best definition.

☐ The amount of money available to pay off long-term debts.

☐ The amount of money that goes towards the day-to-day running of a business.

☐ The profit a business has made.

Statement of Financial Position Questions

Q6   Complete the formula for **net current assets**. Use words from the box.

> current assets   capital   current liabilities   revenue

> .... − .... = net current assets

Q7   Circle the right words in the sentences below.

Current liabilities are short-term / long-term debts.

An example of a current liability is a creditor / a mortgage.

Long-term liabilities take over a month / a year to pay off.

Q8   Which of the following **sources of capital** are **internal** and which are **external**?
For each item, write either **I** for internal or **E** for external in the box.

money from shareholders ☐   money from bank loans ☐

money from leftover profit ☐   money from a mortgage ☐

Q9   The boxes on the left are all types of **asset**.
Draw lines to match the **asset** on the left to the **type of asset** on the right.

cash

company car

office building   current assets

debtors   fixed assets

Penny's
Pizzas

Statement of Financial Position Questions

Q1 Read the sentences below. Circle true or false for each one.

Debtors are people or businesses that owe the business money. **true / false**

Net current assets are fixed assets and current assets added together. **true / false**

Q2 a) What does the **capital section** of a balance sheet show? Tick the best answer.

☐ How a business is funded.

☐ How a business is using its funds.

☐ How much profit a business has made.

b) What does the **assets section** of a balance sheet show? Tick the best answer.

☐ How many staff a business employs.

☐ How much debt a business is in.

☐ How a business is using its funds.

Q3 Circle the correct words in the sentences below.

Net current assets / Net assets should be equal to capital employed.

A bank loan is usually a **long-term / current** liability.

Q4 Helen is a photographer. On 31st December 2012, the value of her **current assets** was £6500, the value of her **fixed assets** was £4450 and the value of her **current liabilities** was £3400.

You can use a calculator for this question.

a) Calculate the value of Helen's **working capital** on 31st December 2012.

Working capital = £ [   ]

$$\text{current assets} - \text{current liabilities} = \text{working capital}$$

b) Calculate the value of Helen's **net assets** on 31st December 2012.

Net assets = £ [   ]

$$\text{fixed assets} + \text{working capital} = \text{net assets}$$

Statement of Financial Position Questions

Q5 Dylan owns a pet shop. When he was filling in his balance sheet on 30th April 2013, his **share capital** was £5250, his **retained profit** was £8500, and he had a **bank loan** of £10 500.

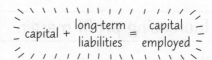
You can use a calculator for this question.

Calculate Dylan's **capital employed**.

Capital employed = £ _____

capital + long-term liabilities = capital employed

Challenge Yourself

Q6 The items on the right need to be entered into the **balance sheet** extract for Jean-Pierre's shoe manufacturing business. Write your answers in the gaps in the balance sheet extract.

You can use a calculator for this question.

	£	£
Fixed assets		
....		....
Current assets		
....	....	
Debtors	4200	
....	....	
Total current assets		....
Current liabilities		
Creditors	400	
....	....	
Total current liabilities		....
Net current assets		....
Net assets		....

Stock £1200

Overdraft £500

Business vehicle £8000

Cash £450

Use these formulas to help you.

current assets − current liabilities = net current assets

net current assets + fixed assets = net assets

Making a Business More Successful

Business owners can compare financial statements to try to improve their business.

Increasing net profit

Most businesses' priority is to try to increase net profit — they can do this by:

Increasing profit margin

1) A business can try to make its products more profitable. It can do this by:
   - increasing the sales price of its products.
   - reducing how much it costs to make the product.
2) Both these strategies are risky.
   - If a business increases the price of its products, its sales may drop.
   - If sales drop too much, the business might not be able to afford all of its expenses.
   - A business might reduce the cost of making a product by using cheaper materials.
   - If the materials are too cheap, sales may drop because customers might think the quality of the product isn't very good.

Reduce expenditure elsewhere in the business

1) A business can increase its net profit by reducing its spending.
2) For example, a firm could rent a cheaper office.

Case study — income statement

Trading, Profit and Loss Account Tariq's Toys Ltd. Year ended 31st March	2013	2012
Sales	99 126	74 412
Cost of sales:		
Opening stock	29 726	14 665
Purchases	43 752	41 021
	73 478	55 686
Minus closing stock	27 797	29 726
Cost of sales	45 681	25 960
Gross profit	53 445	48 452
Minus expenses:		
Wages and salaries	31 000	25 000
Office rent	17 520	7951
Total expenses	48 520	32 951
Net profit	4925	15 501

1) This is an income statement for Tariq's Toys. It compares the business's finances from 2012 and 2013 side by side.
2) Sales have increased in 2013. But net profit, on the other hand, has decreased.
3) This is because the business's cost of sales, wages and salaries, and office rent have risen.
4) To increase its net profit, the business could consider these options:
   - increase the sales price of its products.
   - reduce its cost of sales by finding a cheaper supplier.
   - cut back on office rent by finding a cheaper building to rent.

Making a Business More Successful

A business can use a balance sheet to see if it is using its money efficiently.

Improving balance sheets

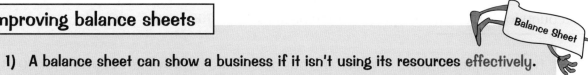
Balance Sheet

1) A balance sheet can show a business if it isn't using its resources effectively.

2) For example, it might show that a business has lots of extra stock, customers that owe the business money or unused assets like machinery.

3) The business can try to turn these resources into cash.

4) It can do this by selling the extra stock, encouraging customers to pay their debts and by selling or renting its unused assets.

5) This money can then be used to make the business more successful.

6) For example, the money might be used to pay off the business's liabilities (what they owe) or it might be reinvested into the business.

Case study — balance sheet

IMGEphotos 31.03.13	£	£
Fixed assets		
Delivery van		5000
Current assets		
Stock	800	
Debtors	4200	
Cash	300	
Total current assets	5300	
Current liabilities		
Creditors	900	
Working capital		
(Net current assets)		4400
Net assets		9400
Financed by		
Share capital		6100
Retained profit		1500
Long-term liabilities		
Bank loan		1800
Capital Employed		9400

1) This is a balance sheet for IMGEphotos for 31st March 2013.

2) The balance sheet shows that the business has some stock, and it's also got a small amount of cash which can be used to pay its day-to-day costs.

3) The business has a lot of money owed to it from debtors. This is money that could be invested in the business, but can't because the debtors still owe it.

4) The business owes money to creditors.

5) So IMGEphotos could encourage its debtors to pay sooner.

6) This would benefit IMGEphotos because it would have more money available to pay off its creditors.

7) It would also have more money to reinvest in the business.

Making a Business More Successful Questions

Q1 The table below shows some information from an income statement (profit and loss account) for 2012. The **net profit** for the business is **£7000** for the year.

Give **two** examples of ways in which the business could **improve** its **net profit** for 2013.

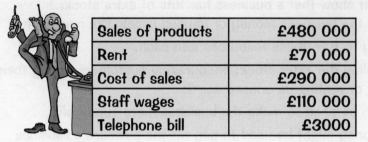

Sales of products	£480 000
Rent	£70 000
Cost of sales	£290 000
Staff wages	£110 000
Telephone bill	£3000

Example 1: ....

....

Example 2: ....

....

Q2 The table below shows some information from a **balance sheet** on 31st October 2012.

Give **two** examples of ways in which the business could **improve** its position.

	£	£
Fixed assets		
Business vehicle		1500
Current assets		
Stock	600	
Debtors	2000	
Cash	400	
Total current assets	3000	
Current liabilities		
Creditors	650	
Overdraft	1500	
Total current liabilities	2150	
Working capital		
(Net current assets)		850

Example 1: ....

....

....

....

....

Example 2: ....

....

....

....

....

Making a Business More Successful Questions

Challenge Yourself

Q3 a) The extracts below are taken from BATSS Ltd's **balance sheet** and **income statement**. Using the words from the boxes to help you, fill in all the missing information.

Net profit	Total long-term liabilities
Capital employed	Gross profit

You can use a calculator for this question.

Balance sheet for BATSS Ltd	(2012) £	(2011) £
Financed by:		
Share capital	52 500	54 725
Retained profit	15 250	10 589
Long-term liabilities		
Mortgage	4500	7500
Bank loan	9800	11 250
....	....	....
....	....	....

Income statement for BATSS Ltd	(2012) £	(2011) £
Income from sales	104 521	105 655
Cost of sales	65 060	38 970
....	....	....
Total expenses	25 500	22 750
....	....	....

b) From the extracts above, was BATSS Ltd **more financially successful** in **2012** or **2011**? Support your answer with some **evidence** from the extracts above.

....

....

Answers

Section One — Businesses and Costs

Page 7

1) false — Start-up costs are usually only paid once.
2) false — Raw materials are an example of a direct cost.
3) Any one from, for example, rent / staff wages / raw materials / utility bills
4) £1000

Pages 8-9

1) a) office rent
   b) raw materials
2) Any two from, for example, cooking ingredients / packaging / delivery costs
3) a) start-up cost
   b) operating cost
   c) operating cost
   d) start-up cost
4) variable cost per unit × number made/sold = **variable costs**
   fixed costs + variable costs = **total costs**
5) a) £120
   b) £670
6)

	1000 items sold
Variable costs	£20 000
Fixed costs	£5000
Total costs	£25 000

Page 11

1) false — Other people as well as other businesses can buy shares.
2) true
3) Revenue is all of the money that a business receives.
4) true

Pages 12-13

1) receives, Selling products or services, Buying shares in another business
2) a) selling extra resources, investing money in high interest bank accounts
   b) advertising products
3) Payments from customers, Selling unwanted furniture
4) true, false, true
5) revenue = **number of sales** × **price per unit**
   or
   revenue = **price per unit** × **number of sales**
6) a) £10 000
   b) £50 000
7) Revenue from crime novels = 950 × £7.50 = £7125.
   Revenue from cookbooks = 1100 × £10 = £11 000.
   Total revenue = £7125 + £11 000 = **£18 125**.

Page 14

1) false — Money spent on electricity bills is an example of revenue expenditure.
2) Any one from, for example, rent / electricity bill / water bill / gas bill / telephone bill / management salaries

Page 16

1) succeed, expenditure, Overheads, rent
2) advertising
3) true, true, false
4) rent, maintenance of website, telephone bill

Page 17

1) greater, less, negative
2) **revenue − expenditure = profit**
3) £20 000
4) a) Ice cream revenue = 10 000 × £1.50 = £15 000
      Ice lolly revenue = 5000 × £1 = £5000
      Total revenue = £15 000 + £5000 = £20 000
      Profit = revenue − expenditure,
      so profit = £20 000 − £20 150 = **−£150**
   b) a loss — it is a negative value.

Section Two — Planning for Success

Page 19

1) false — The break-even point is where the lines for total costs and total revenue cross.
2) The break-even point is when the amount of money spent on making the product is the same as the amount of money made from selling the product.
3) target or actual sales − break-even point = margin of safety

Pages 20-21

1) a) true
   b) false — At the break-even point, a business hasn't made a profit or a loss.
   c) true
   d) false — At the break-even point, a business hasn't made a profit or a loss.
2) a) 250 units
   b) 100 units
   c) 200 units
3) Answer c) — The difference between the target or actual sales and the break-even point.
4) a) break-even point
   b) before
   c) after
   d) total costs
   e) the same point where the fixed costs line starts
5) The vertical axis shows the costs and revenues.
   The horizontal axis shows the units sold.
6)

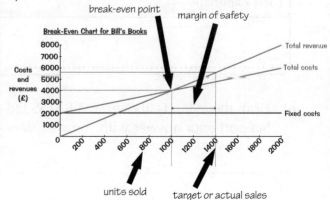

Answers

Page 23

1) false — The 'total costs' line always starts at the fixed costs line.

Pages 24-25

1)

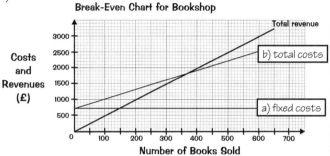

Break-Even Chart for Bookshop

c) 350 books
d) £2500
e) 600 books

2) a)

Number of units sold	Variable costs (£)	Fixed costs (£)	Total costs (£)	Total revenue (£)
200	600	1500	2100	1600
300	900	1500	2400	2400
400	1200	1500	2700	3200
500	1500	1500	3000	4000
600	1800	1500	3300	4800

b) 300 gnomes

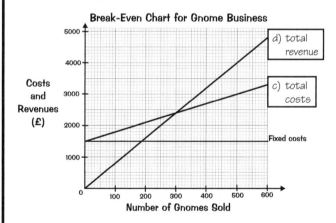

Break-Even Chart for Gnome Business

Page 26

1) false — It shows the loss-making area.
2) variable costs

Pages 28-29

1)

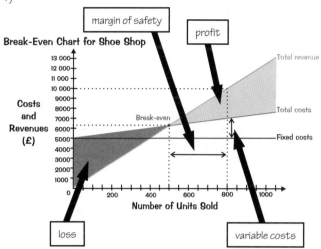

Break-Even Chart for Shoe Shop

2) loss, profit, Total costs
3) a) true
   b) false — If the fixed costs decrease, the break-even point will be lower.
   c) true
   d) true
4) If the sales price increases the break-even point will decrease. If the sales price decreases the break-even point will increase.
5) Answer c) — More customers may be attracted to the product.
6) a) His break-even point will increase to 750 units.
   b) He will need to sell more products to cover his costs, or sell the products at a higher price.

Page 31

1) true
2) false — It must sell more to make a profit.
3) true
4) They would be more likely to reduce their selling price to beat the competitor's price and attract new customers.

Pages 32-33

1) a) false — Break-even analysis cannot predict if customers will like a product.
   b) true
   c) true
   d) false — Break-even analysis can't show if a bank will give a business a loan — it can only be used to help persuade a bank to give it a loan.
2) a) business
   b) break-even
   c) units
   d) increase
3) to attract more customers
4) a) a bank
   b) new
   c) a good investment
5) To make more profit, a business might try to cut costs.
6) a) costs
   b) least
   c) more

Answers

7) It will be unable to check if its target sales are achievable. It will not know when it will start making a profit.

8) Any two from, for example, so that it knows how many products it needs to sell to cover its costs / so that it can judge whether its costs are too high / so that it can prevent a loss / so that it can see how its costs will affect its profit or loss.

Page 35

1) false — It predicts how much a business will spend over time.
2) Budgeting involves predicting figures and setting limits, whereas budgetary control compares these budgeted figures against actual figures.

Pages 36-37

1) A plan of how much money will go in and out of a business.
2) office rent, stock, staff wages
3) revenue, market research, advertising campaign
4) a) true
   b) false — Limits are set to stop a business spending too much.
   c) true
   d) true
5) A business may end up with more money than budgeted if better advertising is used.
   Budgetary control is when budgeted figures are compared with the actual figures.
   Variance is when there is a difference between the actual figures and budgeted figures.
   A business may have less money than expected if costs increase.
6)

Month	Budgeted Revenue (£)	Actual Revenue (£)	Variance
January	10 000	9000	(1000)
February	12 000	13 000	1000
March	12 000	11 000	(1000)

7) supplier problems

Page 39

1) Any two of, for example, sale of products / sale of assets / interest payments / borrowed money

Page 41

1) Cash deficit means that a business does not have enough money to cover its outflows.
2) Cash surplus means that a business has extra money in its account above what it needs to cover its day-to-day outflows and an amount set aside for unexpected costs.

Page 42

1) A prediction of all the money going in and out of a business over a period of time.
2) Inflow — money going into a business
   Closing bank balance — opening bank balance plus the net cash flow
   Net cash flow — inflow minus the outflow
3) a) true
   b) false — Sales of assets are an irregular inflow.
   c) false — Irregular outflows are more difficult to predict than regular outflows.

4) Ask customers to pay by cash.
   Arrange a credit period with its suppliers.

Page 43

1) Arrange a short-term loan.
2) Invest in new resources.
3) a)

	January	February	March
Total inflow (£)	5000	5000	4000
Total outflow (£)	2000	2000	3000
Net cash flow (£)	3000	3000	1000
Opening bank balance (£)	1000	4000	7000
Closing bank balance (£)	4000	7000	8000

   b) The business will have made a surplus, so could reinvest the money into the business by introducing a new product or expanding the business to make even more profit.

Page 45

1) true
2) Any one from, for example, it can predict if a business will have a deficit / it can predict if a business needs to arrange a loan / it can predict if the business will have long-term cash flow problems

Page 46

1) timings, survive, delay, selling, credit
2) a) Organise a loan
   b) Any one from, for example, the business will need a loan for a longer period of time, i.e. from January to April rather than just February to March / the business will need to borrow a larger sum of money / the business will need to arrange a loan sooner, i.e. by January

Page 47

1) a) funds
   b) loans
   c) repay
   d) should
2) decisions, machinery, capital, money, surplus
3) a) true
   b) false — Not making a cash flow forecast doesn't guarantee a business will have a deficit.
   c) false — It could still get a loan, however, it might be more difficult to persuade a bank to give them a loan without evidence that the business should be able to repay them in the future.
   d) true

Page 49

1) false — Net cash flow is the difference between the total inflow and the total outflow for a given month.

Answers

Pages 50-51

1)

	June	July	August	September
Sales revenue (£)	300	700	600	600
Other inflows (£)	100	0	0	0
Total inflow (£)	400	700	600	600

2)

	January	February	March	April
Sales revenue	1000	1000	4000	5000
Other inflows	-	-	-	-
Total inflow (£)	1000	1000	4000	5000
Wages and rent	2000	3000	2000	2000
Total outflow (£)	2000	3000	2000	2000
Net cash flow	-1000	-2000	2000	3000
Opening bank balance	2000	1000	-1000	1000
Closing bank balance	1000	-1000	1000	4000

3) a) true
   b) false — It will have a positive bank balance.
   c) false — It won't need a loan at the end of April because it will have a cash surplus.

4) a)

	January	February	March	April
Sales revenue	100	200	200	300
Other inflows	-	-	300	-
Total inflow	100	200	500	300
Wages and rent	200	200	200	200
Other outflows	-	400	100	-
Total outflow	200	600	300	200
Net cash flow	-100	-400	200	100
Opening bank balance	200	100	-300	-100
Closing bank balance	100	-300	-100	0

   b) An advertising campaign
   c) Miranda must arrange a short-term loan or an overdraft for February to April.

Section Three — Measuring Success

Page 53

1) true
2) false — Positive gross profit can also result in a negative net profit.
3) true
4) Any one from, for example, expand the business / pay shareholders / invest the money / pay bonuses to staff / put money aside in case of unexpected costs

Pages 54-55

1) **revenue − cost of sales** = gross profit
2) a) £6500
   b) -£1500
   c) Classic-Cars was financially unsuccessful because its gross profit was negative, meaning the business was operating at a loss.
3) Net
   Gross
4) **gross profit − expenditure** = net profit
5) a) £1500
   b) £1250
6) a) £19 000
   b) £9000

Page 57

1) true
2) in the bottom section
3) gross profit
4) false — It is found in the top part (the trading account).
5) true

Pages 58-59

1) profit and loss account, smaller, top
2) a) opening stock
   b) net assets
3) gross profit, Sales, raw materials, purchases
4) Rent
   Opening stock
5) a) false — Income statements are usually based on financial information over one year.
   b) true
   c) false — 'Revenue' is money a business receives, but 'cost of sales' is money that a business has to spend to make (or obtain and sell) a product.
6)

	£	£
Income from sales		54 300
Cost of sales	15 600	
Gross Profit		38 700
Expenses		
Office expenses	1050	
Advertising	1200	
Total expenses	2250	
Net profit		36 450

Page 61

1) false — Depreciation is the loss in value of an asset over time.
2) true
3) Any one from, for example, debtors / stock / cash
4) Any one from, for example, share capital / profit that has been reinvested into the business

Answers

Page 63

1) false — It's only valid for the day it's written.
2) true
3) net current assets

Pages 64-65

1) ...how much it owns.
   ...what it owes.
2) debtors
3) bank loan, overdraft
4) cash — A, machinery — A, money owed from customers — A, money owed to suppliers — L, mortgage payments — L, stock — A
5) The amount of money that goes towards the day-to-day running of a business.
6) **current assets** – **current liabilities** = net current assets
7) short-term, a creditor, a year
8) money from shareholders — I, money from bank loans — E, money from leftover profit — I, money from a mortgage — E
9) current assets — cash, debtors
   fixed assets — company car, office building

Pages 66-67

1) true
   false — Net current assets are current assets minus current liabilities.
2) a) How a business is funded.
   b) How a business is using its funds.
3) Net assets, long-term
4) a) £3100
   b) £7550
5) £24 250
6)

	£	£
Fixed assets		
Business vehicle		8000
Current assets		
Stock	1200	
Debtors	4200	
Cash	450	
Total current assets	5850	
Current liabilities		
Creditors	400	
Overdraft	500	
Total current liabilities	900	
Net current assets		4950
Net assets		12 950

Pages 70-71

1) Any two from, for example, increase the sales price of its products if it believes sales won't be affected much / reduce how much it costs to make (or obtain and sell) its products / reduce its business expenses
2) Any two from, for example, encourage its debtors to pay their debts sooner so it can invest the money back into the business / pay off its creditors so it has fewer liabilities / pay off its overdraft so it has fewer liabilities

3) a)

Balance sheet for BATSS Ltd	(2012) £	(2011) £
Financed by:		
Share capital	52 500	54 725
Retained profit	15 250	10 589
Long-term liabilities		
Mortgage	4500	7500
Bank loan	9800	11 250
Total long-term liabilities	14 300	18 750
Capital employed	82 050	84 064

Income statement for BATSS Ltd	(2012) £	(2011) £
Income from sales	104 521	105 655
Cost of sales	65 060	38 970
Gross profit	39 461	66 685
Total expenses	25 500	22 750
Net profit	13 961	43 935

b) BATSS Ltd was more successful in 2011 because it had a higher net profit, meaning the business was more profitable.

Glossary

assets	What a business owns and what is owed to it. Assets can be fixed (for example, a company vehicle) or current (for example, cash or stock).
break-even	When a business has made enough revenue to cover the cost of sales.
budgetary control	When a predicted budget is compared with actual figures.
budget	A prediction of the money going in and out of a business. This might include a limit on the money spent.
capital	The money that funds a business.
capital employed	All the money that has been invested into a business.
cash flow forecast	A financial record that predicts when money should be coming in and going out of a business.
cost of sales	The cost of making or obtaining and selling a product.
creditor	Someone that a business owes money to.
debtor	Someone that owes a business money.
direct costs	Costs that directly relate to making a product, for example, raw materials.
expenditure	All the money that a business spends.
fixed costs	Costs a business has to pay even if it produces nothing, for example, rent.
gross profit	The money left over once cost of sales has been taken away from revenue.
income statement	A financial record that shows how a business has performed over a period of time.
indirect costs	Costs that can't be directly related to making a product, for example, a telephone bill.
liabilities	What a business owes to other people or businesses. Liabilities can be long-term (for example, a bank loan) or current (for example, creditors).
loss	When expenditure is greater than revenue.
margin of safety	The difference between target or actual sales and a business's break-even point.
net profit	The money left over once expenditure has been taken away from gross profit.

Glossary and Index

operating costs	Costs paid by a business on a regular basis, for example, staff wages.
overheads	A type of expenditure that needs to be paid even if the business produces nothing.
profit	When revenue is greater than expenditure.
revenue	All the money that a business receives.
start-up costs	Costs a business only has to pay for once when the business is being set up.
statement of financial position	A financial record that tells a business what it owns and what it owes to others.
variable costs	Costs that change depending on output, for example, the cost of raw materials.
variance	The difference between budgeted financial figures and actual figures.
working capital	The money available to pay for the day-to-day costs of running a business.

Index